MW01088689

Printed in the United States of America

First Printing, 2017

ISBN: 978-1-5203202-0-5

Istoria Ministries Press
1112 W. York
Enid, Oklahoma 73703

www.istoriaministries.com

Table of Contents

Introduction to *Radically New*

I am a follower of Jesus Christ. Jesus changed my life radically when, by His grace, I came to embrace the good news of the New Covenant that Jesus came to establish. It's my desire to lead you into the freedom and joy of New Covenant living. *Radically New* is written for that purpose. It is a book many years in the making.

Some compare writing to breathing. Both the best writing and the best breathing flow unhindered and unlabored. Over the course of the past decade, I have often sat at my desk and written articles on the New Covenant. These articles weren't forced, but sprang from within, usually after a verse of Scripture or experience in life caused me to rejoice in Christ and His work on my behalf.

I hope it reads for you as easily as it flowed from me.

Radically New compiles nearly three dozen of my favorite writings in the form of a book. Not every chapter will be as powerfully liberating as others, but every chapter contains a principle of New Covenant living that is worth your reflection.

Little elephants are chained to a stake when trained. These baby elephants unsuccessfully try to remove the stake with a flick of their necks, but they are unsuccessful. It is the elephant's long memory that keeps an adult elephant tethered to a stake. The adult elephant could easily remove the stake from the ground with a simple flick of the adult elephant's strong neck. But the elephant never tries. He remembers that he can't.

We Christians have long memories. We remember childhood Sunday School lessons where our teachers warned us that God rewards good little boys and girls and punishes bad little boys and girls. We remember the religious training of our youth where our youth pastors told us God punishes the sexually immoral. We trembled as we took our pledges of purity to be blessed by God, and hid our failures as best we could. Over time, our Christian religion becomes more about figuring out how to hide and cover up our sins so that we can appear like we are in the good standing with God. By the time we become adult believers in Jesus Christ, we compartmentalize our lives. Church on Sunday. Life the rest of the time. We have remembered so much of our early religious training that we never try to think or live any differently than we've always thought and lived. Our old religious patterns of thought linger.

I want to re-train the way you think and live as a follower of Jesus Christ.

By way of summary, the New Covenant is God's radical New Agreement with sinners whereby He unconditionally promises to love us, favor us, and bless us *simply because we trust His Son Jesus Christ*. In New Covenant living, we trust in the work and performance of Jesus Christ for God's good promises in this life, not our religious efforts or works. The Good News of the New Covenant is for every flawed person, and we are all terribly flawed. Religious people hide their flaws because they try to pretend they are perfect. However, there is nobody who fully loves or obeys God. We are all fractured, and broken people. Those who promise God to be better and trust in their religious performance to obtain God's favor are relying on the principles of the Old Covenant that God had with Israel, as described in the Old Testament.

God reveals the truth of the New Covenant throughout the books we call the New Testament, but Paul best summarizes the New Covenant in in his letter to the Romans:

"The righteousness of God is given through faith in Jesus Christ to all who believe" (Romans 3:22).

That God blesses us because of Christ's obedience and not our obedience is such a profound and life-transforming truth that many Christians haven't even begun to comprehend it.

My wife and I recently enjoyed some fellowship with a woman in her seventies. She was raised Dutch Reformed and is now active in the Presbyterian Church in America and models her life on the principles of the Old Covenant as found in the Old Testament and God's relationship with Israel.

Our friend is a delightful lady, one with whom we enjoyed visiting. However, through the course of our conversation there arose a stark and pointed difference between what she believes and what we believe. She is a "Law person," and emphasized over and over that "God blesses obedience."

Of course, nobody would disagree with her statement *in principle*. God does bless obedience. The question is "Whose obedience?" Our Presbyterian friend seemed to be emphasizing her and her husband's personal obedience. My wife and I will only emphasize Christ's obedience (i.e. "Christ's fulfillment of the Law"), and God's blessings freely given to us because of our *faith in Christ*.

Our friend's views of the Christian life compared to my wife's and mine represents the fundamental difference between Old Covenant Christians and New Covenant Christians.

I am a New Covenant Christian. I am uninterested in turning a sinner into a keeper of the Mosaic Law. I am solely concerned with turning a sinner into a person who trusts and loves Jesus Christ. Jesus told us He came to fulfill the Law and the prophets (Matthew 5:17). He meant it. Jesus fulfilled the Law with His life, death, and resurrection, and then He abolished it. He then *became a new Law Giver for His people*. Jesus said:

*"A new commandment I give to you, **that you love one another, even as I have loved you**, that you also love one another. By this love all men will know that you are My disciples."* (John 13:34-35).

Throughout this book, you will find many examples of the differences between Old Covenant and New Covenant living. The first example of the differences between Old Covenant living and New Covenant living comes from an anecdote I heard given by my friend Jon Zens.

Jon pointed out that the early Puritans in America were Christians who based their lives on Old Covenant principles. They came over to the New World and found themselves facing the Native Americans (Indians) turned to the Old Testament for how they should solve the Indian problem. Old Covenant typology dominated the Puritans behavior toward the Indians.

The Puritans saw their exodus from England paralleling Israel's exodus from Egypt in the Old Testament.

The Puritans viewed their crossing of the Atlantic as a parallel to Israel's crossing of the Red Sea. The Puritans believed that their arrival in the New World paralleled Israel's arrival and entrance into the land of Canaan. The Puritans hoped that the New World would indeed be a land "flowing with milk and honey."

But now came the major mistake the Puritans made because of their emphasis on the Old Covenant.

The Puritans believed that the Native Americans they met in the New World paralleled the heathen nations Israel met in the land of Canaan. How should they respond? Old Covenant typology pointed to casting out the Native peoples by force, precisely as Israel cast out the heathen nations in Canaan.

However, *Christ commands His people in the New Covenant to love their enemies*. Should the Puritans follow the Law of Christ by loving and evangelizing the Indians, or should the Puritans follow the example of Old Covenant Israel and kill the native dwellers?

According to Zens, the Puritans behaved in a manner consistent with their Old Covenant beliefs. Over time they removed or exterminated the Indians, claiming the New World for God.

Many people today who claim to be followers of Jesus may be following Old Israel and the Old Covenant Laws more than they are the New Covenant and the New Lawgiver (Jesus).

Now, back to the Presbyterian lady we met. Her husband was not a believer in Christ. She married him fifty years earlier, and the past five decades were "exceedingly difficult." She desperately wanted her husband to be "obedient" to God's Laws (e.g., worshipping on the Sabbath, tithing on their income, etc.) because "God blesses our obedience."

I was worn out listening to her.

I think what our friend's husband needs is a wife who is so full of Christ, so appreciative of the perfect righteousness that Jesus Christ graciously gives her, that *she loves her husband exactly the way Jesus Christ loves her*. It seems to me that if the New Covenant were the foundation of her theology and philosophy of living, then she would set aside any emphasis on her husband's performance-- or lack thereof -- and simply love her husband without expectations or conditions.

Obviously, this introduction has simplified some very complex issues, but my goal in this book is to encourage you to begin a journey toward New Covenant truths. It's an axiom that if there is maladjustment in one's *behavior* toward people, it's usually because of a problem in one's *belief* regarding the character of God toward sinners.

I'm hopeful that *Radically New* will help you understand and believe God's amazing love toward us in Jesus Christ, and that our Law Giver is the Person of Jesus alone, for He fulfilled the Old Covenant in His life, death, and resurrection.

Jesus abolished the Old Agreement God made with Israel and instituted a New Agreement with the world.

Chapter 1: People Who Read the Bible Often Mistake the End of the Old Covenant with the End of the World

One day the disciples asked Jesus the question: *"Tell us, when shall these things be? And what shall be the sign of Thy coming, and of the **end of the world**?"* (Matthew 24:3). This verse, from the King James Bible, is an unfortunate translation of the question the disciples were asking.

The disciples wanted to know when the age of Temple worship and God's covenant with Israel would come to an end, not the earth.

The word "world" (KJV) is a mistranslation of the Greek word *aeon*. This Greek word is the word from which our English word eon – which means "age" – is derived. So, *aeon* should be translated *age* in Matthew 24:3). But the King James translators, unfortunately, used the English word "world" to translate the Greek word *aeon*. The entire discussion between Jesus and the disciples in Matthew 24 revolved around **when** the Jewish **age** – that is "the Old Covenant" – would come to an end, not when the world would come to an end. Because of this unfortunate mistranslation, many Christians miss the fundamental message of the Bible. Jesus Christ came to earth to fulfill and then abolish God's Covenant with Israel, the agreement we now call "the Old Covenant," and to inaugurate a "New Covenant" with all the peoples of the world.

Jesus had already shocked his disciples by prophesying that the Jewish Temple in Jerusalem would soon face destruction, and "not one stone of the Temple would be left standing upon another" (Matthew 24:1-2).

In response, the disciples asked Jesus "when shall these things be?" They wanted to know when the tearing down of the stones of the Temple would occur. "What will be the sign of Your coming in judgment?" the disciples asked. They knew Jesus believed the Temple to be a "den of thieves," and they knew He intended to judge the religious leaders of the Temple. The disciples asked Him when "*the end of **the age**"* (e.g. the Jewish age) would occur?

Matthew 24 is not a discussion about the end of the world, but a discussion about when God would bring an end to the Covenant He made with the Jews.

When God chose the Jews among all the peoples of the earth, He described His choice to enter into covenant with them in very vivid terms. God "*stretched forth the heavens, and laid the foundations of the earth*" when He chose the Jews as His people (Isaiah 51:13, 16). Throughout the Old Testament, God's covenant with Israel is called "heaven and earth."

When God warned Israel of punishments coming their way for their unfaithfulness to His covenant, He says "*Hear, O heavens, and give ear, O earth*: for the LORD hath spoken, and I have nourished and brought up children, and they have rebelled against me" (Isaiah 1:2). The Lord chooses the language He uses when He communicates with man. God describes His covenant with the Jews as "*heaven and earth*" (see Isaiah 13:13; Haggai 2:6). When God came in judgment upon Israel during Old Testament times (722 B.C.) through the Assyrians, He speaks of "*shaking the heavens and the earth*" (Isaiah 24:1, 19-20).

After many times of "shaking" the "heavens and earth" (e.g. the Jews), Jesus told His disciples in A.D. 30 that the Jews covenant with God would one day come to an end. He says "***Heaven and earth will pass away****, but my words shall not pass away.*"

(Matthew 24:35). The Jewish age, the Old Covenant, will come to an end, but the words of Jesus will endure. Of course, Jesus had already made it clear that the Old Covenant ("heaven and earth") would NOT "pass away" until *"every jot and tittle of the Law is fulfilled"* (Matthew 5:18).

Jesus Himself fulfilled the rituals, the ceremonies, the types, the shadows and the Law of the Old Covenant. Jesus is the fulfillment of the Law (e.g. the five books of Moses). All things in the Old Covenant point to Him! After Christ's resurrection, God waited 40 years and then abolished the Jewish *age* (the Temple, the rituals, the sacrifices, etc.).

Why wait 40 years?

In the Bible, the number 40 is the number God uses when making a transition on the earth. Examples include the flood (40 days of rain), the Jews' wandering in the desert before Canaan (40 years of wandering), and the transition into Jesus the Messiah's public ministry (40 days of testing in the wilderness). The language Jesus used in predicting the end of the Jewish age is clear. God will cause "heaven and earth" to pass away. "Heaven and earth" is the very language God used when He selected Israel as His Covenant people among all the peoples of the world (e.g., "I stretch forth the heavens, and establish the earth" Isaiah 51:13, 16).

The disciples wished to know "When?" the Jewish age would end. They needed a time for "heaven and the earth" (the Covenant with Israel, Temple worship, the Law, etc..) to end. Jesus answers their question of "when" by giving signs of His coming in judgment upon Israel (Matthew 24:4-33) and then Jesus makes an astounding statement in Matthew 24:34:

*"**This generation** shall not die until all these things are fulfilled."*

A Jewish generation is forty years, and just as Jesus prophesied, the Romans destroyed the Jewish Temple in A.D. 70 – precisely a generation after Jesus prophesied the end of the Jewish age. The historian Josephus records for us that the Romans tore down the

Jewish Temple by tearing down the stones until not one was left standing upon another. The Jewish Age had come to an end. It was over.

Modern evangelicals would do well to let Scripture interpret Scripture and see the end of *"the heavens and the earth"* as the end of the Jewish age. Frankly, we look silly when we get caught up in the fanciful teachings that try to make Matthew 24 a prophecy about the end of the earth. The Bible is quite clear that the earth will never end. Jesus said *"The meek will inherit the earth"* during His sermon on the mountain and Solomon declared that *"the earth shall endure forever"* (Ecclesiastes 1:4).

Heaven is the earth with the curse fully reversed. When Christ ends this age of grace (the New Covenant) and "folds it up like a garment" (Hebrews 1:10), He will raise the dead and give His people the gift of immortal life. He will unite our eternal home which He's been preparing for us (John 14:1-5) with the earth. The earth is "groaning, waiting for this day of redemption." God redeems all of His creation, not just His people.

We don't know when God will end the church age, but we would do well to realize that many of the passages that modern evangelicals interpret as the "end of the earth" are in reality very specific prophecies about the "end of the Jewish age. " The abolishment of the Old Covenant and the installation of the New Covenant through the Person and work of Jesus the Messiah is the message of both testaments. Christ came in A.D. 70 in judgment upon the nation of Israel and ended the Old Covenant Jewish system of religion and established the New Covenant with all the peoples of the world.

The great Hebrew scholar John Brown understood the radical difference between the Old and new Covenants. Dr. Brown recognized that many Christians are ignorant of the message of the Bible because they've never taken the time to understand the Old Testament. "A person at all familiar with the phraseology of the Old Testament Scriptures knows that the dissolution of the Mosaic economy, and the establishment of the Christian economy, is often spoken of as the removing of the old earth and heavens, and the creation of a new earth and new heavens." (John Brown, vol. 1, p. 170).

Charles Spurgeon once wrote:

> "Did you ever regret the absence of the burnt-offering, or the red heifer, or any one of the sacrifices and rites of the Jews? Did you ever pine for the Feast of Tabernacles, or the dedication of the Temple? No, because, though these were *like the old heavens and earth* to the Jewish believers, *they have passed away*, and we now live under new heavens and a new earth, so far as the dispensation of divine teaching is concerned. The substance has come, and the shadow has gone: and we do not remember it." (Charles Spurgeon, Metropolitan Tabernacle Pulpit, vol. xxxvii, p. 354).

May God deliver us from basing our interpretations of the end of the world on a misunderstanding of Matthew 24.

Chapter 2: The Old Covenant Challenges Your Head, but the New Agreement Changes Your Heart

Every Bible is divided. There are two parts to a Bible. The first part is called the Old Testament and the second is the New Testament. Most people never pause to consider the definition of "Testament." It simply means agreement. When you prepare for death, you complete your "Last Will and Testament," an agreement between you and the state for the disposition of your assets.

A synonym for the word "testament" is "covenant." Again, the word covenant is an archaic word we don't use much anymore. When you fill out paperwork for buying a new home, you may come across a neighborhood "covenant," which is an agreement between you and your future neighbors that nobody in the neighborhood will build, remodel or do anything else in a manner inconsistent with the neighborhood agreement (covenant).

So you could easily say that the Bible contains two "agreements" between God and man - the Old Agreement (Covenant) and the New Agreement (Covenant). These two Covenants are totally different agreements. If you are a believer in Jesus Christ, your take your marching order from the New Agreement, not the Old Agreement.

A big problem in many churches, however, is the manner in which preachers and teachers interpret the Bible. When it comes to the "rule of life" for followers of Jesus Christ, many Christian leaders go straight to the Old Agreement. The interpretative lens through which many Christians read their Bibles and live their lives is through the Old Covenant. However, the proper lens through which we are to read the entire Scriptures and live our entire lives is through the New Testament Scriptures. This New Agreement, inaugurated by the Person and work of Jesus Christ, is vitally important to understand because Jesus "fulfilled" the Old Agreement *and then abolished it.*

That's right. Jesus caused the Old Agreement to disappear (see Hebrews 8:13). Religious people who emphasize the Old Agreement find themselves in bondage because they've missed the beauty of Christ. They have been both "hardened" and "blinded" by a veil that clouds any clear thinking about Jesus. The Apostle Paul put it like this:

> "But their minds were hardened; for until this very day at the reading of the Old Covenant the same veil remains unlifted, because it is removed in Christ. But to this day whenever Moses is read (e.g. the Law), a veil lies over their heart; but whenever a person turns to the Lord, the veil is taken away. Now the Lord is the Spirit, and where the Spirit of the Lord is, *there is liberty.*" (II Corinthians 3:14-17)

Those three verses from II Corinthians should explain to you why people can talk about God and the various agreements (religions) that people have with God and the world will leave them alone. But the moment someone starts speaking of Jesus Christ all hell breaks loose.

The demons of hell leave religious people alone, not to mention those religious leaders who are "the blind leading the blind." But when God's agreement with the world through the Person and work of Jesus Christ is exalted and honored, all hell breaks loose "lest the veil be taken away" and sinners come to rest in the New Covenant between God and man.

Three Major Differences between the Agreements

Though I could point out dozens of differences between the two biblical Covenants (Agreements), I would like to encourage you through three major differences, and then challenge you to make sure you recognize you are part of the New Agreement between God and man and not the Old Agreement.

1). The Old Agreement is filled with conditional promises based on *personal* obedience; the New Agreement is filled with unconditional promises based on *Christ's* obedience and our faith in Him.

When Israel heard Moses read the laws of the Old Agreement they shouted "All this we will do" (Exodus 19:8). However, the narrative of the Old Testament Scriptures is filled with Israel's rebellion to their agreement with God. As a result, their quid pro quo Old Agreement ("If you will," God says, "then I will...") with God, brought all kinds of punishment from God. However, in the New Agreement, Jesus Christ's perfect righteousness in fulfilling the Law obtained all the blessings of God that the Old Agreement Law promised - and Israel failed to obtain by their obedience. Therefore, in the New Agreement, you are blessed by God because of your faith in Christ. Faith is why the New Agreement is called "the obedience of faith" (Romans 16:26). It is why "all the promises of God are "Yes" (a resounding "Yes") in Christ" (II Corinthians 1:20), and not "maybe yes" based on your performance for God or obedience to God.

Many Charismatics base their "prosperity gospel" teaching on Old Agreement Scriptures. They say that "if you tithe" or "if you give your seed" then you obligate God to "bless you" for your obedience. Not true. In the New Agreement, God promises to meet your every need according to His riches in Christ (Philippians 4:19).

God will not meet your need because your obedience measures up. God makes the promise that He will meet "every need" of His people of the New Covenant. He gives a "resounding yes" to all His promises to those who trust the Person and work of His Son.

If you are a member of a church that emphasizes all the conditional promises of the Old Agreement, you will constantly be harangued to measure up. If you are a member of a gospel church, you will constantly be encouraged to grow in grace and your knowledge of the beauty and glory of Jesus Christ (II Peter 3:18).

2). The Old Agreement was filled with *hundreds of laws* that touched every facet of life in the nation of Israel; the New Agreement contains *one Royal Law* that touches every facet of life for the New Agreement believer.

The laws of the Old Agreement were designed to point Israel to the One who was to come. Israel celebrated - by Law - the festivals; all of which were designed to point to Jesus the Christ of God, the inaugurator of a New Agreement between God and man. Israel worshiped God - by Law - though various sacrifices and Sabbaths. Again, all these festivals, sacrifices, and Sabbaths were designed to point Israel to the coming Messiah of God and the Inaugurator of a New Agreement between God and man. Even the prophets who lived during the Old Agreement kept looking forward to the coming of the New Agreement (see Jeremiah 31). Ancient Israel knew that the Law only condemned and it would be the Messiah who would save.

When Jesus came and inaugurated the New Agreement with His blood (i.e. His death, burial, and resurrection), He became the New Lawgiver and gave us just one commandment - a new commandment - which is to encompass every aspect of our life.

*"A **new commandment** I give to you, that you love one another as I have loved you"* (John 13:34).

The nation of Israel could be distinguished as "God's chosen people" through their obedience to the laws of the Old Agreement (e.g. circumcision, Sabbath rest, the laws of the feasts and festivals). So too in the New Agreement, those whom God has chosen from the nations are known by their obedience to the Royal Law of love.

Jesus said, *"By your love for others all men know will know you are my disciples"* (John 13:35).

Instead of a husband looking to a list of how to be a good husband, if that husband would simply love his wife as Christ has loved him - unconditionally, sacrificially, selflessly (without expectation of reciprocation) - husbands would be amazed at the transformation in their marriages. A new agreement believer is full of grace and love because he's come to understand the grace and love of God in Christ for him (see Ephesians 3:14-21).

3). The Old Agreement causes me to look to a list of laws to measure up to *God's expectations for me*; the New Agreement *causes me to look to the Christ* (the Messiah) and marvel at the infinite grace and love of God for me in Jesus Christ.

I love reading the Old Testament. In fact, my favorite studies of all time are expositional verse-by-verse studies of Old Testament books like Exodus, Leviticus, Daniel, Jeremiah, Esther, etc. However, I love those Old Agreement books because I read them through the filter of Jesus Christ and the New Agreement He inaugurated between God and me.

Truth be known, I never see bad things that happen to me as punishment from God - ever. Rather, in the New Agreement, when I enter into the storm, I always see Christ holding out His hand and inviting me to go with Him through the storm because "something remarkably good is on the other side" (Romans 8:28).

The Bible is not a child's book. It is extremely profound. Christianity is not serendipitous, puerile, or childish. I am a Christian because I understand the goodness and riches of God in Christ in the New Agreement, foreshadowed in the Old Agreement. I want to continue to be captivated by the love and grace of God in Christ. Christ is the only One that brings me true life, liberty, and happiness.

I want to rest in Him.

Chapter 3: The New Covenant in the Five "I Wills" of God

*"But this is the covenant that **I will** make with the house of Israel; After those days, says the Lord, **I will** put My law in them, and write it in their hearts; and **I will** be their God, and they shall be My people. And they shall teach no more every man his neighbor, saying, 'Know the Lord:' for they shall all know Me, from the least of them unto the greatest of them, for **I will** forgive their iniquity, and **I will** remember their sin no more."*—Jeremiah 31:33-34

There is a host of problems in the way God's people think about the state of our world today. Many Christians live in fear and bondage because they're looking for something to come instead of faith and boldness in what has already appeared. Evangelicals seem to have little understanding that Christ *"made obsolete and caused to disappear"* the Old Covenant, and He inaugurated a New Covenant through His blood for both Jews and Gentiles alike (see Hebrews 8:13).

Many Christians take demands for obedience to the Law and a call to repent for non-performance of the Law, and they merge these two things (the Law and the Prophets) with the New Covenant message of "love, hope and faith" through Christ's obedience and perfect fulfillment of the Law on our behalf.

A Jesus follower should understand that Christ fulfilled the Law and abolished the Old Agreement. In its place, Jesus has inaugurated for the world a New Agreement. People from every nation, kindred, tribe and family trust Christ for the fulfillment of all the good promises of God to them.

After Jesus had inaugurated the New Covenant through His death and resurrection in A.D. 30, there was a forty-year period of transition for national Israel to move from the old way of relating to God toward the new. This forty-year period (A.D. 30 to A.D. 70) were the *"last days"* of the Old Covenant; for it was *"made obsolete... and was soon to disappear"* (Hebrews 8:13). When the New Testament speaks of *"the last days,"* it refers to *"the last days"* of the Old Covenant demand for obedience to the Law of God to receive the blessings from God.

Obedience in the Old Covenant required Temple worship in Jerusalem; the sacrificial offerings brought to the Temple, and the observance of seven major festivals or holy days (i.e. "holidays"). From AD 30 to AD 70 the Temple still stood. The Jews still brought their sacrifices to the Temple. God's chosen people from the Old Covenant still celebrated the festivals. Most of the early followers of Christ were Jewish, and they preached the good news of Jesus Christ at the Temple in Jerusalem and Jewish synagogues throughout the land and even participated in the Jewish Temple festivals.

John, the writer of Revelation, writes to encourage these early Jewish Christians that though they were about to see *"the end"* of everything Jewish. John reminds them the Temple in Jerusalem is about to be destroyed. Jerusalem itself would fall. The Romans would extract furious retribution on the Jews as they marched through the valley of Megiddo to destroy the Jewish way of life. John writes to the early followers of Christ to tell them they are never to forget that Jesus is ending their Jewish way of life to establish a New Agreement with the world. God has established His Kingdom over the nations. The "gates of hell" will not prevail against Jesus Christ building His church in this New Agreement. "The end" of the Old was coming; but the New Way of nearness to God through *"the obedience of faith"* (Romans 16:26) was dawning.

Andrew Murray wrote an outstanding book in 1898 called *The Two Covenants* where he says the problem with many Christians is that they come to Christ with an Old Covenant mentality, but never leave it behind. The fear of God, repentance toward God, hope in

God, and promises to change for God are all a part of early Christian living, but Murray believes that continuing in this Old Way of thinking leads to more fear and bondage. The Old Covenant mentality of *"If I obey God, then God will bless me"* (Jeremiah 7:23) will never remove the desire for sin from me. Murray says that every believer in Christ must progress from an Old Covenant way of thinking to a New Covenant way of resting. It is the performance of Jesus Christ that matters, not our own. Jesus perfectly fulfilled the Law, securing all the promises of God's blessings for His people.

But most Christians don't understand what it means to come to Jesus to rest. When Jesus says "My yoke is easy" and "My burden is light," He meant it. Jesus inaugurated a New Way of thinking about our intimacy and closeness with God. I will only draw near to God in full assurance of His love and blessing for me when I see the New Covenant that Jesus established has nothing to do with my performance. In Jeremiah 31:33-34 God reveals to the prophet five things God will do for His people in the New Covenant inaugurated and established by His Son.

Think through God's five "I Wills" and learn to rest in Christ.

1). God will make the covenant for me - *"This is the covenant I (God) will make..."*

The New Covenant is unconditional; it requires no conditions from me. The Old Covenant is a *quid pro quo* covenant, where God "returns one thing for another" (e.g., God's blessing for my obedience). However, the New Covenant is an unconditional agreement where God's gives His grace to me without any conditions on my part, except for faith in His grace to me in Christ and a clear understanding of my unworthiness. "This is a trustworthy statement, deserving of my full acceptance, that Christ Jesus came into the world to save sinners, among whom I am foremost of all" (I Timothy 1:15).

2). God will put His law in me - *"I will put My law in them, and write it in their hearts..."*

Whereas the Old Covenant was an agreement of Law imposed upon a hardened people, the New Covenant is an agreement with the "law of love" impressed upon a softened people. "By this," Jesus said, "will all people know you are My disciples, by your love for one another" (John 13:35). God stamps this internal law of love which onto the regenerate heart. The New Covenant law is clear, given to us by a lawgiver greater than Moses. Jesus said, "A new command I give you: Love one another. As I have loved you, so you must love one another" (John 13:35). This new "law" (command) is "written on my heart." I am compelled to love others for "the love of Christ compels me" (II Corinthians 5:14).

3). **God will be forever with me** - *"and I will be their God..."*

In the Old Covenant God said "Obey my voice, and I will be your God (Jeremiah 7:23 and 11:4). God set conditions on the old agreement, "There are blessings from me if you obey me" (Deuteronomy 11:27). However, in the New Covenant, "if we are unfaithful, He remains faithful, for He cannot deny who he is" (II Timothy 2:13). God's promise to me in the new agreement is that He will "never fail me." He will "never leave me." He will "never abandon me." (Hebrews 13:5). This New Covenant blessing from God, properly understood, keeps me free from the love of money and possessions, as well as anxiety over material things (see Hebrews 13:5).

4). **God will forgive even my intentional sins** - *"for I will forgive their iniquity..."*

A person who murdered someone unintentionally in the Old Covenant could flee to a City of Refuge (Deuteronomy 19:4-12). However, the intentional murderer - the one who "lies in wait in hate" (Deuteronomy 19:11) -- would find no mercy, but was handed over to death by the "avenger of blood." Not so in the New Agreement. Even my sins which are clearly intentional, what the Bible calls iniquity, are completely forgiven by God. "There is therefore now no condemnation to them which are in Christ Jesus" (Romans 8:1). Some might object, "But God can't forgive any future sins which I intentionally commit! He only forgives my past sins for which I'm sorry, and I seek His forgiveness." I ask you, "Which of your sins were future when Christ died and how many of your sins, if any, are truly unintentional?" Forgiveness is through Christ's blood "at-one-ment." In the Old Covenant sin separated the sinner from God; in the New Covenant, the work of Jesus Christ brings an "at one moment" (atonement) between God and sinners.

As long as I measure whether or not I'm intentional in committing sin instead of focusing on God's initiative in forgiving all my sin— intentional or not—I'll never be free from the power of sin. In the New Covenant, I find forgiveness with no conditions by my faith in Christ. My sin is obviously destructive by sin's very nature, but God's gracious New Agreement with me by the blood of His Son ensures my forgiveness.

When you see a sign that says "Wet Paint: Don't Touch" you immediately want to touch it. The law seems harshly imposed. A sign that says "Wet Paint: Feel Free to Touch It But Know That You'll Get Stained" has a tendency to keep you from touching because someone is lovingly and graciously encouraging you to avoid something harmful to you. The first paint sign "Don't Touch" represents the Old Covenant. The second paint sign "Feel Free" represents the New Covenant.

5). God will remember no more my sins - *"and I will remember their sin no more..."*

When God says "I will remember their sin no more," He sets me free to "boldly enter into the presence of God in my time of need" (Hebrews 4:16). God's New Agreement with me through the Person and work of Jesus Christ ensures that my struggles in this life never keep me from closeness with God. Instead of worrying about my performance, I rest in Christ's performance for me.

My deliverance is from the Lord.

Chapter 4: Jesus Christ Fulfilled the Law of the Old Covenant and Established the New Covenant

Leviticus 23 outlines seven feasts that the Lord instituted for His Old Covenant people, the nation of Israel. These seven feasts, called 'The Feasts of the Lord' were the holy days (or holidays) of Old Testament Israel. They were so important that when the Lord commanded Moses to institute the feasts among the Hebrew people, the calendar changed. The month during which the Hebrews observed the first three feasts became the first month of the Jewish year. This month – called by the Hebrew name *Abib* while Canaan, but later called by the Babylonian name *Nisan* after the Hebrews returned from their Babylonian exile (539 B.C.) – is the beginning of the Jewish religious year.

For centuries, including during the times of Christ, all Jewish males would make their way to Jerusalem three times a year to participate in these seven Old Agreement feasts or festivals. The Hebrews would make a trip in the spring to Jerusalem in the spring to celebrate the first three feasts, in the summer to celebrate the fourth feast, and in the fall to celebrate the last three feasts.

The first three festivals in the spring were called *the Feast of Passover, the Feast of Unleavened Bread*, and *the Feast of the Sheaf of First Fruits*. The Hebrews celebrated all three of these festivals during just one week beginning with the 14th day of Nisan (Passover) and continuing for an additional seven days.

During the Feast of Passover, Hebrew families selected a spotless lamb from their flock to sacrifice. The lamb chosen as the Passover Lamb must contain no disease, defect or blemish. The Lamb must also be in its prime regarding age and strength. The Hebrew family would then slaughter the chosen lamb. The blood of the lamb would be sprinkled on the doorposts of the Israeli home, commemorating that night in Egypt when God brought Israel out of their Egyptian bondage. During that night of deliverance from Egypt (see Exodus 12), God killed the first-born son in every Egyptian home, but He'd promised His people he would "pass over" (thus, Passover) the Hebrew homes where – by faith – the Hebrews applied the blood of the lamb.

The Hebrew Passover week during Nisan corresponds to either our March or April on the solar calendar, depending on the year. As you are probably aware, the week of the Feast of Passover is also the same week that Jesus died to "fulfill the Law." Jesus followers call this week Passion Week, referring to the suffering and death of Jesus Christ for sinners. We who have faith in Jesus Christ, who is called "the Lamb of God who takes away the sin of the world" (John 1:29), are promised that God passes over us in judgment for our sins. Jesus Christ fulfills the Law by being the spotless Lamb of God who came as the sacrifice for sinners.

Old Covenant Hebrew families ate the lamb in a meal they called "The Feast of Unleavened Bread." During this time they remembered the grace of God in delivering them from bondage in Egypt. So too, we who have faith in Christ celebrate the Lord's Supper, where we remember the grace of God for us in Jesus Christ. For on the night before Jesus' crucifixion, He took bread and passed it to his disciples and said, "Take and eat, for this is My body which I give for you. Eat this to remember me" (I Corinthians 11:14).

Leaven is a picture of "sin" for an Old Covenant Hebrew. When the Hebrews ate the Passover Lamb, they had cleared their house of all leaven, thus the Feast of Unleavened Bread. During the Feast of Unleavened Bread, Jesus was in the tomb, sweeping away our sins and fulfilling the Law.

The weekly Sabbath for Old Covenant Hebrews is the day we call Saturday. During Passover Week, "on the morning after the

Sabbath" (that is, the day after Saturday during Passover Week), the Hebrew men would all go the Temple and celebrate the third festival of Passover. They would carry with them to the Temple a "sheaf of their firstfruits" from their farms. Before the Hebrew men came to Jerusalem to celebrate Passover, they went to their fields and took a fistful of ripe grain. Most of their grain crop was not yet ripe, so this fistful of grain was called "first fruits." They came to the Temple on Sunday morning and "waved their first fruits" before the Lord and prayed to God that He would bless their entire crop as He had their first fruits.

Of course, it was on this morning – early Sunday morning – precisely when the Old Covenant Hebrew men were "waiving their first fruits" that Jesus Christ rose from the grave, ensuring for all New Covenant believers that God would raise us up from the dead and give us the gift of eternal life. Jesus Christ fulfilled the Old Covenant Law by raising from the dead on the day of the Festival of First Fruits. When the Apostle Paul speaks of believers' future resurrection in I Corinthians 15, he writes, "But now Christ has been raised from the dead, the first fruits of those who are asleep" (I Corinthians 15:20).

The fourth Old Covenant Feast is the Feast of Pentecost. It occurs exactly *fifty days* after the celebration of the Feast of the Sheaf of First Fruits – on a Sunday, too! Pentecost occurred during Israel's spring grain harvest (our May/June), and it pictures the Holy Spirit bringing in the full harvest of God's Kingdom.

The Spirit of God is bringing people from "every nation, every kindred, every tribe, and every family" to faith in Jesus Christ. The harvest, Jesus said, is plentiful, and He came as the first fruits of all that God will do for His people.

The fifth, sixth and seventh Feasts – *the Feast of Trumpets, the Feast Day of Atonement*, and *the Feast of Tabernacles* respectively – occurred during one week of Israel's fall fruit harvest (our September/October), and they also point to the Person and work of Jesus Christ. But right now, I want to look closer at Passion week.

Passion Week or Passover Week

I agree with the great Greek and New Testament scholar B.F. Westcott that Jesus died on Thursday, Nisan 14, the day of the Feast of Passover, was buried and in the tomb during the High Sabbath of Nisan 15 (Friday) which was annually the date of the beginning of the Feast of Unleavened Bread. Jesus remained in the tomb during the regular Jewish Sabbath of Saturday, Nisan 16, and He rose from the grave on Sunday, Nisan 17 also called the first day of the week. In Old Testament language this Sunday, Nisan 17, is called *"the morrow after the Sabbath"* (Lev. 23:15).

Many Christians do not notice that Jesus was in the tomb over *two days*, back to back Sabbaths - on Friday the High Sabbath of Unleavened Bread (John 19:31), and on Saturday the regular Jewish Sabbath. Matthew 28:1 says *"After the Sabbaths* (in the Greek the word is plural), at dawn on the first day of the week, Mary Magdalene and the other Mary went to look at the tomb."

During the Feast of Passover, the Jews eat the roasted lamb, remembering the 'passing over' of God's judgment in Egypt. In Old Covenant days, this week of festivals in the spring commemorates God's grace to Israel through His redeeming them out of the bondage of Egypt. But when you read the Old Covenant Scriptures (the Old Testament), your mind should immediately go to Jesus Christ, and Christ's fulfillment of the God's Law in the Old Agreement.

Easter is all about Jesus Christ fulfilling the Feasts of Israel. He is the Lamb of God who died on Passover day and whose blood (or death), applied to our minds and hearts through trust in Him, causes the judgment of God to 'pass over' us. Jesus is the 'Unleavened Bread' who was in the tomb during the Feast of that name, taking with Him the leaven (sin) of our lives and removing it from us. Jesus took our sins to the grave and cast them as far from us as 'the east is from the west,' and separating us unto God as a holy people. Jesus rose from the dead on the Feast of First Fruits," guaranteeing that we too shall rise from the dead. In the New Covenant which Jesus inaugurated by His obedience, death, and resurrection, "no matter how many promises God has made, they are all 'yes' in Christ" (II Corinthians 1:20).

The Jews knew when a new month dawned, like the first month of the year (Nisan) had dawned, because they had priests assigned to watch for the New Moon. The new moon is the time when the moon goes completely dark, and when the priests saw this new moon, they ordered that the trumpets would blow and Israel would then celebrate a New Moon Festival.

 Of course, during the three lunar months when the Hebrews celebrated the seven Festivals of the Lord would, Old Covenant Israel broke out into even more celebratory praise at the sound of the trumpets, anticipating the coming Feasts (holidays). Sacrifices, grain and wine offerings, and special foods all marked the Old Covenant Festivals of Israel.

We don't do celebrate Old Covenant Feasts anymore. We don't offer sacrifices. We don't celebrate New Moons. We don't practice the Feasts. We don't follow the dietary laws of Old Covenant Israel. All these things were shadows, or pictures, of that which was to come - Jesus Christ.

Jesus the Messiah is the fulfillment of the Old Covenant. He fulfilled the seven Feasts in His life, death, and resurrection.

Jesus is the focus of our faith.

To go back to observing all the shadows of the Old Covenant - including the Sabbath - is like greeting your spouse at the airport after a long absence and pulling from your billfold a picture of your spouse and kissing it rather than embracing the person who is standing in front of you.

Being a Christian is all about embracing Christ and resting in His work for you, and ceasing from any efforts to be "pleasing to God" by your own works. We are made right with God by His grace to us in Christ Jesus and our faith in His grace to us in Christ.

We are justified by grace through faith says the apostles, or as Martin Luther put it in the early 1500's as he sought to reverse the corruption of the institutional church, "we are justified by faith," not by our gifts to the church or any other sacraments.

In A.D. 325 the early Christian fathers separated the celebration of 'Easter' from the Jewish Passover Festival. Easter is now on a fixed Sunday – *the first Sunday after the first full moon after the first day of Spring* – and is unfortunately no longer tied to the same week of the Jewish Feast of Passover.

Every Sunday, but particularly on Resurrection Sunday, we who trust Christ Jesus should celebrate all the gracious promises of God for us in Jesus Christ.

New Covenant living is all about our rest in Him.

Chapter 5: The New Covenant Is Radically New

It's difficult for many Christians to grasp the truth that *we are the church*. The New Covenant church is not a building like the Temple was a building in the Old Covenant. We, the people who trust Christ, are the church in the New Agreement God has with the world.

Anytime I hear of Christians who are "upset with the direction of a church," or "angry with the church," or "tired of the church," I wonder if they truly understand what they're saying. *They* are the church. But it's rare to hear a Christian say "I'm angry with myself," or "I'm tired of myself," or "I'm upset with the direction in my life."

Why is it that so many see "the church" as something other than themselves in union with Jesus Christ?

I think the fault lies with Christian leaders -- particularly us pastors -- who for many centuries have attempted to place churches and church ministries on par with ancient Temple and Old Covenant worship. We build massive church buildings to impress. Religious leaders stain the building's glass windows and decorate elaborately to beautify it. We establish a "priesthood" of authoritative pastors/leaders who separate from 'laity.' Those leaders in charge of the religious institution command congregants to tithe into the storehouse of the institution or risk their belongings being devoured by the devil. We set our programs in stone and make them unalterable and unchangeable, just like Israel's Ten Commandments. The modern church evangelical church looks more like Old Testament Israel than those early followers of Christ who were radically different from the "religious" people of their day.

The early Christians were known for their radical departure from dependence on a worship place, authoritarian priests, and any religious performance through ceremony, holy days or sacrificial 'offerings.' Adolph Safir reminds us of the early Christians radically different lives in his brilliant work on Hebrews:

"The Greeks and the Romans were not merely astonished at, but felt irritated by the worship of the early Christians, who without image and altar, without priests and vestments, appeared to them as atheists, men and women 'without gods' and at times felt threatened by the mysterious power Christians possessed as they rejoiced in suffering and met with calm courage the tortures of death itself" Adolph Saphir.

The crystallization of the institutional church using Jewish modes of worship is not limited to Roman Catholicism beginning in the 4th century AD. Eventually, Baptist churches and other conservative evangelical churches, though historically shouting loudly 'no creed but the Bible,' have come to ignore the New Testament teaching on the nature of the true church and have now:

1). Replicated Israel's hierarchy of priestly authority (calling them pastors);

2). Imitated Israel's emphasis on a particular type of worship at a specific place (calling it sanctuary worship);

3). Perpetuated Israel's obligation to the old 'if-then' covenant with God ('if you obey God fully, then God will bless you liberally').

The freedom of a sinner to personally trust Christ and experience the power of God at work within—transforming that sinner from the inside out - is substituted for a form of behavioral control imposed by a spiritual authoritarian from without (usually a pastor) who uses Old Covenant passages of Scripture to bind believers.

The simplicity of New Covenant worship 'in spirit and in truth' has been overwhelmed by the desires and the demands of leaders within the institutional churches. We pastors, often in an attempt to protect our jobs and salaries (or future jobs and current reputations), spiritualize everything we do, acting as if our ministries and programs are God's ministries and programs. The greatest danger I face at Emmanuel is the temptation to forget that what is done in the building on Sundays and Wednesdays is just a part--a small part--of who we are as a people. When the people live, the Kingdom spreads. The religious institution I lead isn't the Kingdom of God. Whether it is giving, serving, or attending other places of worship, Christ's people should have the liberty and freedom to give, serve, and attend wherever the Spirit leads.

Christ's church *always* leaves the building on Sundays. Therefore the church should never be called the building. Whatever is done on Sundays or Wednesdays in the building should be designed to empower and encourage "the church" (you) to worship in spirit and truth *every day of the week*. My job as a Christian pastor is to lead people in such a manner that they cheerfully give to the Lord, joyfully serve the Lord, and willingly worship the Lord *every day*. A good pastor will always remind God's people that Christ's church extends far beyond the membership rolls of any particular institutional church. If the Spirit leads someone to join another 501 C3 non-profit institution that uses different methodologies and ministries, then great! We Christians are all on the same team. We are all His church.

If the Spirit leads His people to give less, attend less, and serve less at their local non-profit, then the non-profit's budget, ministries, and organizational mission efforts will shrink. If the Spirit leads His people to give more, attend more, and serve more, then the non-profit ministries will expand. Regardless, the New Testament is quite clear that Christ's church is not a new Temple, Christian pastors are not a new priesthood, and God gives liberty to His New Covenant people to follow the Spirit as He leads. Liberty, not Law characterize new Covenant living.

When God's people give, serve and worship as the Spirit leads, where the Spirit leads, and as long as the Spirit leads, amazing things begin to happen. In the New Covenant, it is not the Law that constrains us, but the Spirit who compels us. Unfortunately, many modern evangelical churches have taken promises and laws of the Old Testament and attempted to force them into the New Covenant church. The result is a dysfunctional gathering of law worshippers who are more concerned with conformity than a gathering of strong, individual believers who are empowered by the Spirit.

Or, as I heard my father one time say, "The difference between Christ's people and institutional religion is the difference between reality and pretension. Tears from a broken heart are real, NOT tears in the eyes. Praise from a joyful heart is real, NOT praise from our lips. Rest from a trusting heart is real, NOT rest from our work. Love from a giving heart is real, NOT love from our talk. Institutional religion promotes that which isn't real, but true Christianity encourages authenticity. Who the people of God are in the building on Sunday should be who we are at home or the workplace on Monday."

I can almost hear objections from some pastors who say, "But God has rules about the church! The Word of God prescribes bringing the tithe into the storehouse! The Word of God demands that God's people 'be in submission' to pastors in the church! The Word of God dictates everything we do at our church! God is most interested in what happens at His church! The Word teaches us that our greatest allegiance in life should be to Christ's church, those who shepherd us, and all that the church is doing."

My response is simple: "To which of the two Covenants do you belong?"

In the Old Covenant, everything revolved around the building called the Temple, and the rituals associated with the Temple. In the New Covenant, YOU are the Temple of the Living God (II Corinthians 6:16).

Is the Word from which you receive your marching orders the Word of God pertaining to Israel in the Old Covenant? Or are you looking to the Word of God that pertains to followers of Christ in the New Covenant? Listen to what the writer of Hebrews says about Jesus Christ:

*"When He said, 'A new covenant,' He has made the first (the old) obsolete. **But whatever is becoming obsolete and growing old is ready to disappear.**"* (Hebrews 8:13)

The writer wrote the book of Hebrews around AD 65, thirty-five years after the death of Christ. He writes in Hebrews 8:13 that God's Old Agreement with Israel was made obsolete by the work of Jesus Christ, is growing old and will shortly be abolished (disappear). The Old Agreement God made with Israel is called "The Old Covenant" and is found in the Old Testament. Old Covenant worship revolved around the Tabernacle/Temple, the priesthood, and the festivals and sacrificial rituals (collectively called "The Law" in the OT). The Law was an "if/then" agreement where God promised to Israel His blessings "if" Israel obeyed the Law. The writer of Hebrews tells us three explicit things about this Old Covenant and the "if/then" promises of God that came with it:

1). According to the book of Hebrews, the Old Covenant has been made obsolete.'

2). According to the book of Hebrews, the Old Covenant is 'growing old'

3). According to the book of Hebrews, the Old Covenant was soon to be abolished.

These three biblical truths about the Old Covenant should lead us to ask three questions:

First, when did God's covenant with Israel become obsolete?

Answer: In A.D. 30 Jesus the Anointed One died on a hill called Golgotha. The night before He was crucified He took a cup of wine and declared, "This cup is the New Covenant of my blood shed for the remission of your sins" (I Corinthians 11:25). The next day, on the cross, Jesus cried "It is finished!" (John 19:30). Everything about the Old Covenant-- all the laws, the rituals, the sacrifices and the types--were all fulfilled in Christ. The Old Covenant had served its purpose (as a schoolmaster that points the sinner to Christ) and is now fulfilled. God made it obsolete in the death/burial/resurrection of Christ.

Just like your old television set is made obsolete by the new wave of communication called HDTV, so too, the old pattern of worship in ancient Israel was made obsolete by the new pattern of worship opened up at the cross. The veil was ripped, so the sinner has direct access to God through Christ. And the good news about this new way is that the sinner who comes to God by Christ is guaranteed that he will 'never be cut off from the goodness of God' (Hebrews 7:25). No longer is worship about Temples, priests and rituals. In the New Covenant, those who truly worship God worship Him in "spirit and truth" (John 3:23).

Second, when did God's covenant with Israel grow old?

Answer: For forty years (a Jewish 'generation') after the cross, from AD 30 to AD 70, the Temple remained standing. During those forty years the early followers of Jesus Christ came to the Temple to pray, worship, and proclaim the new way to God through faith in Jesus Christ. It was on the steps of the Temple that Peter healed the lame man by saying, "I have no silver and gold. But that which I have I give to you. *In the name of Jesus Christ rise and walk"* (Acts 3:6). The disciples preached Christ in and around the Temple grounds, but the Old Covenant Temple way of worship was 'growing old.'

So too, after God brought the Apostle Paul to faith in Christ on the road to Damascus, Paul came back to Jerusalem and "preached Christ boldly at the Temple" (Acts 9:27). The Jews were so furious with this former Old Covenant Hebrew who now advocated the New Way to approach God that they sought to have him killed. The disciples thwarted the Jews plan for Paul by secretly escorting the

Apostle out of Jerusalem for his own safety. Old Covenant worship was growing old. The phrase 'growing old' must be interpreted within the context and time of the writer of Hebrews. He was living in the mid-60's AD, and for over three decades since the death of Christ, Temple worship among the Jews continued --but it was growing old and would "soon disappear" (be abolished).

Third, when was God's covenant with Israel abolished?

Answer: In AD 70 God used the Roman army to destroy the Temple. Just as Jesus prophesied forty years earlier (Matthew 24), the Romans did not leave one stone standing upon another. This destruction of Jerusalem and the Temple and the Old Covenant way of worship was prophesied by the prophets and Jesus for centuries. Israel had been unfaithful to the covenant they had with God, and God, therefore, abolished it and instituted a new covenant. Again, it is not as if there was no good purpose for the Old Covenant. If it were not for the Law (the biblical way of describing the Old Covenant), Paul would not have known sin. The Law acted as a mirror, reflecting back to the Hebrews their sinfulness and God's holiness. In addition, the Law, particularly through its festivals, rituals and symbols, portrayed a coming Anointed One (Messiah) who Himself would take away the sins of the world. When the Messiah came and fulfilled the Law, the Old Covenant was made obsolete by God, grew old in time, and was eventually abolished (disappeared) in AD 70. The Temple was gone.

The dwelling place of God in the New Agreement that He has made with sinners, called the New Covenant, is the life of the individual believer. It is the life of God in the soul of man that is the true miracle of the New Covenant. The power of the Spirit of God changes the sinner from the inside/out. We are the Temple of the Living God. For this reason, any institutional church that tries to substitute itself as the old Temple, its pastors/priests as the Old priesthood, and operate by Old Testament "if/then" principles and promises, is denying the truth of the New Testament.

The New Covenant changes the way we worship God every day of our lives. The Old Covenant agreement between God and Israel was a "come see" religion. Come see the Temple. Come see the rituals. Come see the festivals. The New Covenant compels us to "go tell" others the good news. We go tell sinners of the Savior who has guaranteed the Creator's goodness to those who trust Him. Christianity is radically spiritual, internal, personal, and trans-cultural (all people). Some of the best worship you can have is with family or a small group of believers around a camp fire at a lake, or at home around the dinner table, or at a backyard barbecue. Believers are the church. God dwells in us. Where we are, there He is. We don't behave one way 'at church' and another way everywhere else. We can't do this because we ARE the church. Further, since the life of God is in the individual sinner who trusts Christ, there is no hierarchical authority in the church. Every believer is a priest unto God.

The New Covenant changes the way we apply Scriptures from the Old Testament. The "If ... then" Scriptures are seen as part of God's promises to the people of Israel. Let me give you three examples of "if/then" promises that Christian people use wrongly.

(Example 1) *"If My people, which are called by My name, shall humble themselves, and pray, and seek My face, and turn from their wicked ways; then will I hear from heaven, and will forgive their sin, and will heal their land"* (II Chronicles 7:14).

That is a great Old Covenant promise. Israel often failed this condition of humble repentance, and as a result, they were often taken captive by foreigners and their land was destroyed. This verse, often quoted by Christians, is not a New Covenant promise.

In the New Covenant God says that He "is able to do far more abundantly beyond all we even ask or think, according to the power that works within us" (Ephesians 3:20). This is the New Covenant promise. When you come to God by faith in Christ, God resides within you and has begun a good work in you which He will carry to completion. Do you find yourself pulled toward addictive sins as a believer? He will eventually break you of them for your good and for His glory. The alcoholic who comes to God by faith in Christ need not worry that a relapse into drunkenness will cause the favor and goodness of God to withdraw from Him. In the Old Agreement he should have worried, because in the Old Agreement it was his obedience that ensured God's goodness, but in the New Covenant it is God's goodness to Him in Christ that ensures the sinners' eventual obedience.

God is conforming, and He will continue to conform, every sinner who trusts Christ into the image of His Son. It is a guarantee dependent upon His fidelity and strength, not your own.

(Example 2) *"If you bring the tithe ... then I will rebuke the devourer for you"* (Malachi 3:10).

This is an often quoted Old Covenant promise by pastors, used as an enticement (and/or threat) for the New Testament believer to give to his or her local church. This promise, given to Old Covenant Israel, is another if/then promise. The rebuke of the devourer is given IF Israel brings their tithes to the Temple. If the people of Israel do not bring their tithe to the Temple, then the devourer is free to reign and destroy their possessions.

In the New Covenant, Jesus died and in His death He "destroyed the devil" (Hebrews 2:14). In the New Covenant, the devil will seek to devour you as a 'roaring lion,' but as Bunyan so eloquently pictured in Pilgrim's Progress, the lion is chained. Naturalists also tell us that only toothless lions roar. The truth of the New Testament is quite clear. The "strong man" (Satan) who was once at peace in his home (your life) and was well armed, was disarmed and dislodged by One "stronger than he" (Jesus Christ) who has now taken up residence within you (Luke 11:21-22).

As a New Covenant believer in Christ you don't give money to your local church in order for God to rebuke the devourer. Malachi 3:10 is an Old Covenant promise. The devourer is already REMOVED from your life. Jesus is now your Lord. You give as you follow the leadership of the Holy Spirit. The more you comprehend the work of Christ on your behalf the more you cheerfully give, the more you joyfully serve, and the more you radically worship! In other words, in the New Covenant, giving is a matter of the heart, not the Law. As the Spirit leads you to give to ministries that proclaim the good news of Christ, care for the needs of fellow man, and work hard to do kingdom work--then give!

(Example 3) *"If you call upon me in the day of trouble; then I will deliver you"* (Psalm 50:15).

Again, that is a great Old Covenant promise, but it is nowhere close to the incredible truth of the New Covenant Scriptures. In the New Covenant, God delivers His people even when they find themselves emotionally, spiritually and personally "dead in our trespasses and sins" (Ephesians 2:1).

His amazing and aggressive love for His people through Christ ensures that He will "never, no never, no never" (five negatives in the original) leave us or forsake us (Hebrews 13:5). It is interesting that in the first portion of Hebrews 13:5 it says that we should have "the kind of character that is free from the love of money BECAUSE God will never leave us or forsake." We do not live this way IN ORDER for God to never leave us or forsake us. Words are important.

In the New Covenant our lives are a response to God's goodness to us in Christ. In the Old Covenant, people lived their lives in order to obtain God's goodness. If you ever find yourself being motivated to do something in order to get God to do something in return, you are living under the principles of the Old Covenant. Unfortunately, the Old Covenant, and Old Covenant churches, and Old Covenant promises will always let you down. However, the new agreement that God has with sinners will never let you down.

"He is able to save to the uttermost (i.e. a guarantee that you will never be cut off from God's goodness) those who draw near to God through Him" (Hebrews 7:25).

My desire in this book is to turn upside down your understanding of "the church."

Chapter 6: The Old Covenant Glory Has Faded into Oblivion, but the New Covenant Is Eternal

"Moses used to put a veil over his face so that the sons of Israel would not look intently at the end of what was fading away" (I Corinthians 3:13).

The other day Rachelle and I were eating at our favorite Italian breakfast eatery when the owner of the restaurant pulled up a chair and chatted with us. He loves the people of Emmanuel and all we do for the community and missions worldwide. He attends a small church that "celebrates the Old Covenant feasts" and worships "on the Sabbath (Saturday)." He explained that it would be impossible for his family to worship at Emmanuel until we offered a worship service consistent "with the law of God" (i.e. "Sabbath keeping").

We really enjoyed the fellowship with this local Christian businessman, and we respected his convictions, but his words got me to thinking about the commonplace legalism in churches that emphasize differing aspects of the Old Covenant (i.e. "Sabbath keeping," "tithing," "patriarchy," "quiver-full theology," "kosher eating," etc...). It seems to me that the emphasis on "law keeping" by many Christians is akin to Moses hiding God's glory by the imposition of a veil. The Apostle Paul tells us that Moses "didn't wish the people to see that the glory was fading."

Initially, Moses placed the veil on his face to "help" the people. Exodus 34:30 tells us that the people "were afraid" of Moses' shining face because he had been with the Lord. The presence of

God in our midst often brings discomfort, not comfort. To comfort the people, Moses put a "veil" (garment) over his face to "hide the glory." But Paul tells us that the veil ended up hiding the fact that "the glory was fading."

So it is with religious laws, traditions, and rituals. They may have been instituted for benevolent, good reasons. But that which initially comforts God's people winds up hiding the fact that God's glory is gone. The only way to be sensitive to the presence of God is to resist the temptation to build a mechanism (tradition, ritual or law) intended to hide the fact that God is not present. In other words, we Christian leaders ought to do everything in our power to facilitate freedom and liberty among God's people. When people are free—truly free (i.e. the veil or the law is removed)—it's easy to see the evidence of the Spirit's power and presence.

But many of us--instead of celebrating, facilitating and enjoying this freedom that Christ brings--try to hide the absence of the glory of Christ's presence in our midst by imposing religious laws. Second Corinthians 3:14 directly compares the veil of Moses to religious people attempting to impose Old Testament "laws" on Christ's people. Christian people, like Israel, often seem afraid of the power and liberty that comes from experiencing the presence of God. It scares us. We need to keep control of God's people by imposing religious laws.

We need to maintain authority over our religious environment by spiritualizing our comfortable traditions, exalting our static rituals, and demanding conformity to our personal peccadillos rather than depending on God's people to simply spend time with Jesus to hear God themselves. We want all our people to give the same, dress the same, talk the same, look the same, act the same, and be the same. We feel more comfortable with the Law than we do the Spirit. The veil diminishes the glory of God in the individual's life.

"But where the Spirit of the Lord is there is liberty" (II Corinthians 3:17). II Corinthians 3 forms the foundation for Christians never needing to fear what it means for all God's people to experience the real, meaningful and full freedom that comes through abiding

in Christ's presence. New Covenant believers will resist any imposition of religious laws on God's people. We will view all religious "laws" as a veil used to hide the brilliance of Christ's glory in our lives.

When a person, a family, a Christian group or a church all begin to experience the surpassing glory of Christ, things begin to happen that can only be explained by the power of His presence. I hope to share a few narratives in the next few chapters that illustrate the glory of New Covenant living as compared to Old Covenant Christianity.

Chapter 7: Be in Awe of Jesus in the New Covenant and Love Yourself because of His Love for You

I have a two-fold request for you.

First, read again **the title** of this chapter.

Second, mentally set aside any preconceived notions you have of what it means to be a Christian. I am about to blow away everything you've ever been taught by mainstream religion. You should know my standard of truth is God's word, not religion or the opinions of man. My allegiance is to Jesus the Anointed One, Emmanuel Himself, God among us. My allegiance is not to a church, denomination, religion, or any confession of faith, either historical or current.

My allegiance is the Jesus Christ and the incredible agreement God has made to those who trust Him.

So here we go.

Contrary to what you've been taught in church, the measure of your adoration of Jesus, and the only way you will ever truly love others, *is to love yourself.*

Now I know that most Christian teachers try to make you think that you are nothing but a worm; a vile, wretched sinner that causes God to want to puke when He thinks of you. I know that the institutional church has sought to ingrain within you a feeling that you must perform to get God to like you. *Because of the dogmatic assertion that you are worthless, churches define spirituality, preachers claim spiritual authority, and both churches and preachers demand your conformity.*

Yet when Jesus was approached by a young Jewish attorney and asked "Teacher, what is the greatest commandment in the Law?" Jesus responded, "Love the Lord your God with all your heart and with all your soul and with all your mind. This is the first and greatest commandment. And the second is like it: 'Love your neighbor as yourself.' All the Law and the Prophets hang on these two commandments" (Matthew 22:36-40).

According to Jesus, if you do not love yourself, you will be unable to love your neighbor. More importantly, it is impossible to love God "with all your heart and with all your soul and with all your mind" until you are captivated by God's love for you. Everyone knows from personal experience that real, genuine heartfelt love is drawn from a heart that is being loved! The soul that is loved unconditionally, radically, faithfully and steadfastly is magnetically drawn to love in return. Until a human being comprehends God's radical love in Jesus, a human being will never radically love God through an understanding of God's love for us in Jesus. We will only love Him because we understand He first loves us.

Don't misunderstand. There is a subtle difference between loving yourself and demanding others love you. Loving yourself means you are free from the pressure that others love you. What does it matter if others reject you if Jesus loves you and you love yourself? Demanding others love you is a tell-tale sign that there is actually no self-love. Crazy as it may seem (I call it "upside-down-wisdom"), *the more you **seek** love from someone else the less you love yourself.* I am only truly able to love myself when I comprehend the unconditional, eternal, and very person love of God for me. New Covenant believers resting in the love of God through the Person and work of Jesus Christ will give love selflessly to others because we are full of a comprehension of God's almost incomprehensibly great love for us (see Ephesians 3:14-21).

I propose to you the reason the institutional Christian church often leads members to personal bondage is because followers of Jesus have never been captivated by God's love. Coming to a deeper knowledge of this love may come through an understanding of a remarkable truth found in an often overlooked verse in Hebrews. Many would say John 3:16 is the most important verse in the Bible – and without doubt, John 3:16 is beautiful – but I propose that Hebrews 8:13 is the most important verse of Scripture because you can't fully appreciate the love of God mentioned in John 3:16 until you comprehend the glorious truth of Jesus in Hebrews 8:13.

"When He (Jesus) said, *'A new covenant,'* He has made the first obsolete. But whatever is becoming obsolete and growing old is ready to disappear." (Hebrews 8:13)

The night before Jesus died, He took a cup of wine and said to His disciples that this wine represented His blood which is shed so a "New Covenant" (agreement) might be made between God and His people. Jesus came to shed His blood to cause "the first (covenant)" to grow "obsolete" and eventually "disappear."

Wow. *Think about that!*

The first covenant, that is the Old Covenant with Israel (found in the Old Testament), Jesus caused to become obsolete and disappear. Everything in the Old Covenant--Temple worship, the male priesthood of Israel, sacrifices, the feasts and festivals of Israel, the Law, and all other things associated with Israel's ritualistic worship of God in the Old Covenant—became obsolete and disappeared because of the person and work of Jesus.

Jesus Christ "fulfilled the Law," every jot and tittle of it, and then abolished it. There are no longer any Temple rituals. The Law of Israel is obsolete. There is no Sabbath day anymore. Believers find there rest every day in Jesus. The people of God are no longer the Hebrew people only; every ethnicity forms His people. The priests of God are no longer just males, for females share in the eternal priesthood. The Temple of God is no longer in Jerusalem, for "you are the Temple of the Holy Spirit." The festivals are no longer in effect for Jesus fulfilled the festivals. Jesus abolished and caused to disappear the "Old Covenant" with Israel.

Then what good purpose does the Law (Old Covenant) serve? The Old Covenant is the shadow that points you to the appearing of Jesus Christ, and it is the "schoolmaster" that takes you by the hand and leads you to be taught by the Teacher. Jesus' miraculous birth, sinless life, substitutionary death, and powerful resurrection cause you to see HE fulfilled the Law for you. You come to see your absolute inability to be righteous before God by your conformity to any Law, and you come to rest by faith in Jesus! If you read the Old Testament and see a set of laws for you to keep, then you have missed Christ and the New Agreement He instituted with His blood. If you ask, "But what motivates a believer to love people (and therefore not steal, not envy, not lie, etc...)?" I respond, "It is the comprehension of the love of God for your soul through Jesus which translates into loving yourself, which spills over into loving others as you love yourself" (II Corinthians 5:14). Being in awe of Jesus leads to loving yourself.

Any pastor who takes Old Covenant rituals and practices and brings them into the New Covenant, slapping Christian terminology on those Old Covenant rituals and practices, is deceiving believers and leading them away from 'the rest' that comes through faith in Jesus Christ's work. For example, if you've been taught that the church building is "the Temple of God," then you have been misled. The person who comes to rest in the work of Christ is the Temple of the living God. Everywhere you go, God is, because the life of God is in you.

If you've been led to believe that if you don't give 10% to your church then you are "stealing from God," the pastor of your church is misleading you. God actually owns all that you have, and you are but a steward of it all. Give as the Spirit of God leads you, wherever He leads you, because the institutional church this side of the cross is not the Old Covenant Temple of God prior to the cross.

If you have been led to believe that only males can be teachers and proclaimers of truth and that only men can lead, then you have been duped into believing that the Old Covenant principles of male priesthood are still in effect, and you have missed the New Covenant principle that every believer, whether male or female "is a priest unto God." If you have been taught that there are people with "spiritual authority" over you, then you have never seen the truth that Christ alone possesses all authority in the New Agreement and dispenses His authority through the gifts of the Spirit and the servant acts of His people, not the positions and titles bestowed by fellow man.

Jesus Christ ended the Old Covenant and initiated a New Agreement. That's the purpose for which Jesus came. Forty years after the first Passover, Israel entered into Canaan. Forty years after the Lamb of God died at Calvary at Passover (fulfilling the Law of Passover in His death) the Temple in Jerusalem and all Old Covenant rituals were destroyed so that believers in Jesus entered totally unhindered into their spiritual rest.

The Law that was "soon to disappear" in Hebrews 8:13 God made officially *obsolete* in A.D. 70 with the destruction of the Temple. Daniel (in his scroll), Jesus (in His Matthew 24 prophecy) and John (in the book of Revelation) all predicted the same thing: The Old Covenant would come to an end through God's judgment and divorce of the Hebrews for their infidelity.

But the wonderful Good News is that God did Himself what no sinner can do. To be a Christian simply means you enter into an eternal rest through faith in what Jesus did for you and become so overwhelmed by the love of God, that you love yourself BECAUSE God loves you and you begin to love others as you love yourself in Jesus.

Hang your hat on this: If God Himself came to die for you, if God Himself gave His life for you, if God Himself shed His blood to redeem you, if God Himself—the God who flung the stars and holds the earth in its orbit—if this God deemed you worthy of coming to earth, fulfilling the Law in your place, dying in your stead because of your sin, then the love of this God in the death of Jesus should be sufficient enough to convince you that you are indeed someone very, very special. I propose to you that only when you are utterly captivated by what Jesus has done for you will you become overwhelmed with the value, worth and dignity of your person.

If God loves you, then nobody and nothing can separate you from His eternal love. If God loves you, then it is truly unbelief to deny His love. If God loves you, then to hate yourself is to hate God. God died for you while you were yet a sinner, but it is the love of God for your sinful soul that makes you valuable. God loves sinners, not the self-righteous.

Therefore, the man or woman who hates himself cannot love others. But the man or woman who becomes captivated by the love of God in Jesus Christ cannot help but love himself. Ironically, when you love yourself deeply, you are able to love others radically.

Therefore, stop performing and start trusting Jesus. Stop condemning yourself and start loving yourself. Stop slapping Christian terms on Old Covenant rituals and start wrapping your arms of faith around Jesus. The radical love of God is seen in Jesus coming to make the Old Covenant obsolete and causing it to disappear.

He's done that - so now rest in Him and love yourself.

Chapter 8: Lift Up Christ to Sinners and Refrain from Hammering Them with Law

Many conservative evangelicals want to ensure that the world knows it is guilty and going to hell. The philosophy that drives our evangelism is "make sure all people know they are guilty sinners before we ever give to them the good news of Jesus Christ." For this reason, the starting point and greatest emphasis in evangelism for many conservative Christians is the universality of sinfulness.

Or, to put it more precisely, the conservative Christian seems more concerned that the sinner knows he's a sinner than he is that the sinner sees the glory and goodness of God in the person and work of Jesus Christ. The idea clung to by conservative evangelicals is that "the law" must condemn before the Lawgiver can save. This leads the soul winner to bypass proclaiming the goodness of God in the risen Christ until the sinner has been worked over really good with the law and to produce the feeling of condemnation. Sounds legitimate, right?

Well, not so fast. One of the reasons I absolutely love the heritage given us by 17th century English Baptists is because they held to a radical emphasis on simply preaching and proclaiming Christ—leaving the work of conviction and conversion to the Spirit. You can't read the old works of our forefathers without being saturated with the goodness and grace of God in Christ Jesus. We Baptists have historically been supremely Christocentric. Our ancients were not as concerned that the sinner knew and felt his sin as they were the sinner realized experientially the goodness of God in the person of Jesus Christ. This is how they put it in the First London Confession of Faith (1644):

Article 25 in the 1646 London Confession of Faith

"The preaching of the gospel to the conversion of sinners, is absolutely free; no way requiring as absolutely necessary, any qualifications, preparations, or terrors of the law, or preceding ministry of the law, but only and alone the naked soul, a sinner and ungodly, to receive Christ crucified, dead and buried, and risen again; who is made a prince and a Savior for such sinners as through the gospel shall be brought to believe on Him." John 3:14, 15, 1:12; Isa. 55:1; John 7:37; 1 Tim. 1:15; Rom. 4:5, 5:8; Acts 5:30, 31, 2:36, 1 Cor. 1:22, 24.

The starting point for these 18th Century Baptists was the goodness of God in Christ, not the sinfulness of man. "For it is the goodness of God that leads to repentance" (Romans 2:4). Christ fulfilled the Law of God. The Law and the prophets in the Old Testament all pointed to Christ. The Law was never given to drive a man to be righteous in himself, but rather to drive the sinner to faith in the Lawgiver to provide a righteousness that comes from outside the sinner's own obedience. The feasts, the Sabbaths, the festivals, the sacrifices, the laws of Israel, the Temple, the priesthood, and all the other important features of the Old Covenant were realized in Christ.

With the establishment of the New Covenant, signed and sealed by the blood of Christ, the Old Covenant faded into oblivion because it possessed a fading glory, but the goodness and grace of God in the person and work of Jesus Christ has an eternal glory (I Corinthians 3:7-18).

So the next time you hear someone yell and scream and berate the sinner with words of judgment and condemnation, please know that the he/she is neither speaking in a manner that focuses the listener on the centrality of Christ and His goodness which leads sinners to repentance, nor is he being true to his calling as a New Covenant follower of Jesus Christ.

If one objects, "But Christ spoke harsh words of condemnation to the Pharisees in Matthew 23!" I respond: Christ reserved His words of condemnation to the religious who deemed themselves righteous and far superior to sinners. Were we conservative Christians to be biblical in our evangelism we would do two things:

1). We would always proclaim the finished work of Christ to sinners while showing them grace, kindness and love while they are sinners—for it is the goodness of God and the Spirit alone (not the law) that leads sinners to repentance, and
2). We would never complain when the media, the world or cultural liberals ridicule and condemn Southern Baptists for what they perceive as our self-righteousness because self-righteousness is the very thing Christ Himself condemned the Pharisees for having.

Isn't it odd how we get things reversed? We want to yell and scream at the world for its sin, and yet we also get angry and feel the victim when the world yells and screams at us for our self-righteousness. Maybe if we simply loved sinners and proclaimed Christ all the shouting at sinners would stop.

Someone might ask, "But how does a person know he is a 'sinner' without the Law?" Answer: Mankind's refusal to reflect the image of his Creator in being kind and doing good things for others (e.g. "Natural Law") predates the giving of the Mosaic Law, and as such, it is unnecessary for the Mosaic Law to be used in order press home man's condition. Truth be known, mankind is 'dead' in trespasses and sins, not through God's fault, but by Adam's (man's) free choice.

Therefore, what is needed is not for a good man to be convinced of his sin, but for a dead man to be raised to life. The only Law necessary for any person to hear and understand he is in need of deliverance, is the Law that God commands all men to always and consistently without interruption "do good" for others, and always think of other people first. This is what our Creator would have us do (see Romans 2). Jesus called this "The Golden Rule." But there is no person who lives like this, and even worse, none of us is able to change.

Until Jesus Christ changes us from the inside out.

The reason I am a follower of Jesus Christ who identifies as a 'Baptist' is because the theology of my Baptist forefathers (not so much today) is the theology to which I identify. I cling to the New Covenant, my freedom in Christ, and the importance of loving the ungodly in the same manner He has loved me.

Chapter 9: "Heaven and Earth Has Passed Away" for the New Covenant Has Come

Andy Stanley, in his excellent book *Deep and Wide*, writes "People who go to church are not on a truth quest. They are interested in what works." By "what works" Andy means what makes people happy, or what makes life work better.

I agree. People want what works. Yet, in my opinion, what actually works—what actually brings people real happiness and a fully functioning life worth living—is "truth!" Jesus said to His followers, "You shall know the truth, and the truth will set you free" (John 8:32).

Imagine! An addict wishes to be free from addiction - know the truth. A worrier wishes to be free from paralyzing anxiety - know the truth. A divorcee wishes to be free from feelings of rejection and abandonment - know the truth. A man or woman who has failed morally wishes to be free from guilt - know the truth.

The reason churches often seem lifeless is because we go down wrong roads in our quest for happiness and functional living. It isn't our performance for God that works. It isn't tithing that works. It isn't my promises to be better that works. It isn't moral behavior and religious character that works. It isn't personal discipline that works. It's truth.

People need truth and simply don't know it. Worse, Christian leaders called to guide people into truth are often ignorant of it themselves. We become "the blind leading the blind" (Matthew 15:14).

For example, when Jesus said, "Heaven and earth will pass away, but my words will never pass away" (Matthew 24:35), Jesus was not predicting the destruction of the earth on which we live or the disappearance of the starry heavens above our heads.

Likewise, when Jesus said, "For truly I tell you, until heaven and earth disappear, not the smallest letter, not the least stroke of a pen, will by any means disappear from the Law until everything is accomplished" (Matthew 5:18), Jesus was not prophesying the end of the earth.

Many Christians miss the powerful and freeing truth behind Christ's words about "heaven and earth" because they assume this phrase in the Bible refers to the global sphere that orbits the sun (the earth) and the atmospheric heavens above. They're not even close.

Jesus uses the phrase "heaven and earth" to describe God's covenant with Israel (the Old Covenant). With this definition of 'heaven and earth' in mind (and in a moment I'll prove it), a summary of what Jesus was saying in Matthew 24:35 and Matthew 5:18 would be:

*"The Old Covenant ('heaven and earth') will be fulfilled by Me and then it (i.e. 'heaven and earth') will disappear, but **My words** will abide forever."*

That's exactly what Jesus did in His first advent. He came to fulfill the Law, and then He 'abolished' it. He came in order to institute a New Covenant (the 'new heaven and the 'new earth'). He caused the old "heaven and earth" to pass away. The covenant with Israel is now gone. It has actually disappeared (Hebrews 8:13).

The New Covenant is here.

Nobody argues that we no longer bring animals for sacrifice, celebrate the festivals, or follow the dietary restrictions found in the Old Testament. But many miss the most powerful impact of

Christ causing 'heaven and earth' to disappear. Any sinner from any nation can now fully and personally experience God's blessings via faith in Christ.

Under the New Covenant in which we live, God no longer says, "Obedience to my Law brings you blessings" as He did in the former covenant with Israel. Now He says, "Faith in My Son, regardless of your nationality or ethnicity, brings you all My eternal blessings. I will credit you the perfect righteousness of My Son in exchange for your faith and trust in Him."

Jesus perfect obedience to the Law merited complete and personal blessings from the Father. Yet, God graciously promises all those same blessings to those who embrace His Son. Jesus fulfilled it; we faith it.

This truth changes the game of life. But before I show you how the game changes, let me prove the phrase "heaven and earth" refers to God's covenant with Israel and "a new heaven and a new earth" refers to the New Covenant He has in Christ.

'Heaven and Earth' and the Choosing of Israel

When God describes how He chose Israel "among all the nations of the earth" He says, "I have put My words in your mouth and have covered you with the shadow of My hand, to establish the heavens, to found the earth, and to say to Zion, 'You are My people.'" (Isaiah 51:16 NAS). God calls choosing Israel as His people 'establishing the heavens' and "founding the earth." Thus the covenant with Israel itself is called by God "heaven and earth."

When Moses, Israel's Lawgiver, assembled the covenant people of God (Deuteronomy 31:30), he speaks to Israel and says, "Listen, you heavens, and I will speak. Hear, you earth, the words of my mouth" (Deuteronomy 32:1). Moses spoke to the people of Israel, not the literal heavens and earth.

When Israel broke their covenant with God, the Lord sent judgment to Israel through the Babylonians and said "(the earth) is utterly broken down, the earth is clean dissolved, the earth is moved exceedingly...the earth shall reel to and fro like a drunkard, and shall be removed like a cottage; and the transgression thereof shall be heavy upon it; and it shall fall, and not rise again" (Isaiah 24: 1, 3, 4, 19, 20). Israel, again, is called "the earth."

God's choosing of Israel as a favored nation, God giving His Law to Israel for their obedience, and everything else associated with God's covenant with Israel is labeled throughout the Bible as God forming "heaven and earth." It would therefore make sense, that if God was going to end this conditional covenant with Israel and institute a New Covenant with the entire world through faith in His Son, then God would speak of the destruction and abolishment of this first covenant as the "destruction of heaven and earth." This is exactly what He does.

The writer of Hebrews, anticipating the fall of Jerusalem, the destruction of the Temple, and the official end of the Old Covenant system of worship uses this precise language. He writes in Hebrews 12:26-28:

"And His voice shook the earth then (the giving of the Law), but now He has promised, saying, "YET ONCE MORE I WILL SHAKE NOT ONLY THE EARTH, BUT ALSO THE HEAVEN." This expression, 'Yet once more,' denotes the removing of those things which can be shaken (the Old Covenant), as of created things, so that those things which cannot be shaken (the eternal New Covenant) may remain. Therefore, since we receive a kingdom which cannot be shaken (Christ's eternal kingdom), let us show gratitude."

Likewise, when John anticipated God's judgment against Israel through the destruction of Jerusalem and the Temple, bringing to an official 'end' the covenantal system of worship we read about in the Old Testament, he wrote of God removing the old "heaven and earth" (Revelation 21:1) and establishing "a new heaven" and "a new earth" (the New Covenant). In this new agreement between God and the people of the world, God takes a new Bride (people from every nation, not just Jews), forms a new priesthood (every believer, both male and female, not just a tribe of men), establishes a new nation (all believers in Christ are called God's 'holy nation' in I Peter 2:9), and institutes an eternal and unshakable kingdom!

Daniel, John and the other biblical prophets, including Jesus Himself, wrote mostly about the end of God's covenant with Israel and the establishment of the unshakable kingdom of Christ. You and I have received this kingdom. It is within us. It's advancing all around us. One of these days, every enemy of the eternal kingdom will be made Christ's footstool (Hebrews 10:13).

Jesus Christ will return at the end of this New Covenant age of grace (Acts 1:11). He will raise the dead, both the righteous (those who believe in Him) and the unrighteous (John 5:28). Jesus Christ will then call on the unrighteous to give an account for everything they've done in this life (Romans 2:6). The judgment He dispenses for their sins will be personal, equitable and proportional (Romans 12:19).

Those who are 'in Christ' by faith had their sins judged at the cross and will not give an account to God for their sins at the general judgment. Rather, those 'in Christ' are made 'co-heirs' with Christ and inherit a universe where the curse has been finally and fully reversed by the redemption in Christ (i.e. heaven). These end of age things are all true and good, but they are little discussed in the Bible.

Most of the Bible is about God destroying "heaven and earth" (His covenant with Israel) and establishing a "new heaven and new earth" (the New Covenant with the world). When we miss the impact of Jesus Christ coming to "fulfill the covenant of Law" and then causing it to "pass away," by misinterpreting the phrase "heaven and earth" we remain in bondage to Law and our performance to it. The only thing that 'works' and brings 'real happiness' is the Truth that Jesus Christ came to set captives free! He came to destroy 'heaven and earth' and to establish the New Covenant that is 'a new heaven and a new earth' (Revelation 21).

As Charles Spurgeon said:

"Did you ever regret the absence of the burnt-offering, or the red heifer, of any one of the sacrifices and rites of the Jews? Did you ever pine for the feast of tabernacles, or the dedication? No, because, though these were like the old heavens and earth to the Jewish believers, they have passed away, and we now live under a new heaven and earth, so far as the dispensation of divine teaching is concerned. The substance is come, and the shadow has gone: and we do not remember it." (Metropolitan Tabernacle Pulpit, vol. xxxvii, p. 354).

Application

It is an unfortunate occurrence when evangelical church leaders take the principles of the Old Covenant (which have been abolished), slap Christian terms on them, and then try to bind people to full obedience to church laws, promising God's blessings if they obey them and God's curses if they do not. That's not the good news Jesus Christ brings. The truth—the Good News—that brings life, happiness and freedom to anyone with confidence and trust in the Person and work of Jesus Christ is as follows:

First, Jesus Christ has fulfilled the Law in my stead, and as a result, I am considered by God to be perfectly righteous "not because I have a righteousness that comes from my obedience to any law, but because I have a righteousness that comes from God and is found by faith in His Son" (Philippians 3:9). The truth is God sees no sin in me.

Second, Jesus Christ has fulfilled the Law in my stead, and as a result, all the blessings of God are mine, not because of my obedience to any law, but because "He shall supply all my needs according to His riches," not mine (Philippians 4:19). The idea that God blesses me 'when' I give to the church, or 'when I bless Him,' or 'when I (fill in the blank)' is no more the good news of the gospel than Islam, Buddhism, or any other 'ism' built on man's alleged attempts to appease God. The truth is God needs no gift from me.

Third, Jesus Christ has fulfilled the Law in my stead, and as a result, everything in my life that I need will be freely given to me by God. "For if God did not spare giving us His Son, how shall He not freely and graciously give us all things we need?" (Romans 8:32). Sometimes God will allow me to hit rock bottom in order for me to see that He is the Rock. Unlike the Old Covenant where there were conditions on God hearing my prayers (II Chronicles 7:14), petitions for what I need now are always heard by God because the Holy Spirit is always interceding for me during my times of weakness (Romans 8:26). God never ceases loving me and works all things for my good (Romans 8:28). The truth is God always works all things for good—my good.

Finally, Jesus Christ has fulfilled the Law in my stead, and as I begin to grow deeper in my trust and confidence that Jesus is who He says He is and He does what He says He will do, then I can't help but go out and love people in the same manner He has loved me! This is the Royal Law of Jesus. The words of Jesus, which endure forever, clarify the Royal Law. This is my New Covenant law - "To love other people in the same manner He's loved me" (John 13:35). The truth is God sends His love through me.

The way I live as a New Covenant believer in this world:

a). I accept people in sin as if they had no sin, for Jesus sees no sin in me.

b). I freely give what others need, expecting nothing in return, for all I need I have in Jesus and I receive it via simple faith in Him, not by my performance or obedience to Him.

c). I will love others and do good, for my God and Savior Jesus Christ is all the time loving me and working all things for my good.

The way I would live if I failed to see Jesus bringing an end to the Old Covenant way of life:

a). I would always point out the sin and failure of others in conforming to God's laws (however those laws may be defined), because God always judges my failures of obedience.

b). I would do for others what I could, but I would expect others to do something good in return, for God's blessings to me are in proportion to my obedience to Him.

c). Though I would say I loved people unconditionally, I would really only love people based on their abilities to keep the expectations I have for them, for though God truly loves me, He is only pleased with me when I perform as He expects.

Old Covenant living wears people out. It is lifeless and requires a great deal of guilt and shame for people to continue in it. Jesus came to destroy the Old Covenant way of life.

It is only when we begin to see the truth of who Jesus is and what Jesus has done that we begin to experience true freedom. Jesus is the Truth (John 14:6). Jesus came that we might live life to its fullest (John 10:10). Andy Stanley may be right; nobody is on a quest for truth, for everybody is looking for what works. However, ultimately, the only thing that works is Truth.

To whatever extent you are looking forward to the Second Advent of Jesus as an escape from this life, you have missed the impact and power of Jesus's coming in His First Advent. He came to put an end to the Old Agreement of God's blessings based on a sinner's obedience to Law. He came to destroy "heaven and earth."

And now the good news. "If anyone is in Christ, the new creation has come. The old has passed away, the new is here!" (II Corinthians 5:17). It's a new way to live. It's a new way to love. It's a new way to enjoy life to its absolute fullest!

Thank God the 'new heaven and new earth' has come. As it is written, "By faith, the just shall live!" (Hebrews 10:38).

Chapter 10: Women Are Free to Lead Out, Speak Up, and Serve Him in the New Covenant

I find it stunning that anyone who professes to believe in Christ's teachings and the infallibility of the Bible refuses to allow women to teach men, or forbids women from leadership positions, or demands Christians serve (or not serve) their King and His Kingdom according to their gender instead of their giftedness. I am shocked because this is so contrary to the teachings and ministry of Jesus in the New Covenant He came to establish.

Some of my Christian friends, usually men, will respond to me saying, "Listen, Wade, I simply believe and teach the Bible! And as long as I believe the Bible, I can't have a woman be in leadership over men, or have her teach men, or allow her to hold any church leadership position because the Bible forbids it."

That's not accurate.

The Old Covenant religion of the Hebrews did forbid women in the role of worship priest. But of course the Old Covenant also forbade the eating of pork, made Sabbath-breaking (Saturday, not Sunday) a capital offense, and forbade a host of other actions, rules that have "faded away and disappeared" (Hebrews 8:13). Jesus made the former covenant "obsolete" and instituted a New Covenant in His blood, and made us all proclaimers of this new Way of life which is led by the Spirit (II Corinthians 3:6). In this New Covenant age, men and women serve the King and His Kingdom according to their giftedness, not their gender.

But again, my friends who say they believe the Bible will challenge me by quoting I Corinthians 14:34-35.

"The women are to keep silent in the assembly; for they are not permitted to speak, but are to subject themselves just as the Law also says. If they desire to learn anything, let them ask their own husbands at home; for it is improper for a woman to even speak in the assembly." (I Corinthians 14:34-35)

They will then sit back triumphantly and declare, *"There you go! As long as I believe the Bible, I can't ever have a woman in leadership. The Bible means what it says!!"*

Not so fast. My father has brilliantly pointed out the fallacy of this kind of thinking:

"Someone is going to say 'The Bible means what it says.' But that may be the problem. I don't think the Bible means what it says as much as it means what it means and some interpretation must go into understanding its meaning. This would certainly indicate that we need to recognize the possible fallibility of our understanding of Scripture to stay away from the heat that sometimes happens in discussing it."

I want to prove that I Corinthians 14:34-37, in its entirety, derisively dismisses the Old Covenant Hebrew practice—a practice still in vogue in Paul's day among that Jews in Corinth—forbidding women from even speaking in the presence of other men during an assembly. This I Corinthians 14 passage can only be understood in light of what happened to Paul when he visited Corinth (A.D. 50-51), the textual context of the passage itself, and the overall teachings of Christ and His apostle in the New Covenant. You may believe you know what these Corinthian verses say, but I'm asking you to discover what they mean.

Rachelle and I have personally visited Athens, Corinth, Ephesus, Philippi, Berea, Smyrna, Philadelphia, Sardis, Laodicea, Thyatira, Thessalonica and almost every other city or island where Paul traveled during his three missionary journeys. Paul was put on trial in the city of Corinth. He stood before a bema where the Roman proconsul Gallio listened to the accusations of Paul's fellow Jews.

These practicing Jews were not Christians, and they sought to convince Gallio that Paul was persuading people to worship God contrary to the law of God" (Acts 18:13) That's a serious accusation against a Jew; and Paul was a Jew. But the Roman proconsul Gallio refused to make a judgment against Paul saying, "I am unwilling to be a judge of these matters" (Acts 18:15).

Gallio recognized that the conflict in Corinth was a Hebrew religious matter, not a Roman political problem. He did not even intervene as Sosthenes, a convert to Christ through the ministry of Paul as well as a leader in the Corinthian synagogue, was seized and beaten by the Jewish mob before the bema (see Acts 18:17). Paul was hurried out of the Corinthian marketplace while Sosthenes was being beaten by the Jews. Paul was eventually secreted out of the city by fellow believers because of the Jewish threats against him (see Acts 18:18).

Many Bible-believing Christians pay little attention to the accusations Paul faced from the Jews in Corinth during his 18-month stay in the city (A.D. 50 to A.D. 51). The Jews sought to imprison him because of his influence among the people. When they failed to have him arrested, the Corinthian Jews beat Sosthenes for believing what Paul taught. The Roman proconsul Gallio did not prosecute Paul under Roman law as the Jews wanted. Gallio was "unconcerned" with the Jewish religious matters, even allowing the Jews to beat those who believed Paul's religious message (Acts 18:17).

Notice, again, the reason the Corinthian Jews gave to the Roman proconsul Gallio for their anger against Paul - "he is persuading people to worship God contrary to the Law of God." The Law of God is what we now call the Old Covenant and all the practices of Hebrew worship found in the Old Testament and Hebrew traditions. A simple principle regarding our worship of Jesus Christ during this New Covenant age can be logically derived from reading Acts 18 and Paul's time in Corinth:

"The more our corporate worship looks like Old Covenant Jewish worship (i.e. "a holy building in which to gather, authoritative male priests who rule over others, and a sacrificial system of actions designed to please God, etc...), *the more our corporate worship is unlike Paul's and early believers' worship of Christ."* (Wade Burleson)

In one of Paul's earliest epistles, he clearly teaches that in the New Covenant there should be no difference between males and females in the ecclesia (Galatians 3:28), and he later writes to the Corinthian Christians and says all believers should serve one another as they have been gifted (I Cor. 12:4-11). Paul teaches the Corinthians that members of the assembly, both male and female (e.g. all of you), should participate in congregational worship (see I Cor. 14:31 and 14:39), and that women should publicly pray and gifted women should teach others in the ecclesia just as men should publicly pray and gifted men should teach others in the ecclesia (see I Cor. 11:5).

The entire discourse of Paul's writings to the early churches in Greece and Asia Minor is saturated with the new instruction that God's new priesthood is composed of males and females, slaves and free, Jews and Gentiles. In the ecclesia (assembly) of Christ there is to be no separation of people by race, nationality, gender or color. Each of us has been made a priest (Revelation 1:5) and we all form a royal priesthood (I Peter 2:9). These principles radically alter service in Christ's Kingdom, making qualifications for Kingdom service the Spirit's giftedness, not the person's gender.

The Jews who were worshipping in the synagogue of Corinth, however, were greatly offended by Paul's teachings. They heard it with their own ears! Paul was "persuading people to worship God contrary to the Law." This could not be allowed! After the Corinthian Jews had dragged Paul before the bema to charge him with a crime and then beat Sosthenes in the public square, Paul escaped to Cenchrea and then Ephesus (see Acts 18:18).

He later writes to the Corinthian church and was quite blunt about those Corinthian Jews and Judaizers who were infiltrating the church and causing him trouble. He calls them "false apostles" and "deceitful workers" (II Corinthians 11:13), and he tells the Christians in Corinth to resist their false practices and to stand firm to the new "traditions" that Paul had taught them (see I Corinthians 11:2).

Paul reminded them that the practice of empowering all followers of Christ to serve God as the Spirit gifts them—regardless their gender, economic status, or ethnicity—was as precisely why the Jews zealous for the Law in Corinth dragged Paul before Gallio and why Paul had to escape the city. This is the context one should always have in mind when reading the letters of I Corinthians.

So, the startling prohibition of I Corinthians 14:34-35 seems discordant and unconnected to what Paul taught the Christians in Corinth as well as the entire first letter of encouragement he writes to the Corinthians. Look at these two verses again:

"The women are to keep silent in the assembly; for they are not permitted to speak, but are to subject themselves just as the Law also says. If they desire to learn anything, let them ask their own husbands at home; for it is improper for a woman to even speak in the assembly." (I Corinthians 14:34-35)

There's a very good reason why this seems discordant and unconnected to what Paul taught Christians in Corinth and every other city he visited to establish the new Way—it is! I Corinthians 14:34-35 is a quotation of what the Jews zealous for the Law taught about women in the assembly (synagogue), and not what Apostle Paul taught. Because Paul opposed the Jew' position in Corinth on women and worship, and because he taught a new Way in the New Covenant - the Corinthian Jews and Judaizers brought Paul up on charges of blasphemy before the bema.

 So when Paul later writes to the Corinthian Christians (I Corinthians), he knows that all the Christians were familiar with the problem he had in Corinth, that they knew what the Jews taught about women, and they had heard him refute their teaching for 18 months. The Christians in Corinth were all very familiar with the new "tradition" that Paul taught regarding the equality of women in the New Covenant, So he quotes what the Corinthian Jews taught about women in the synagogue (vs. 34-35), and then derisively dismisses it in the next two verses (vs. 36-37) just as he did during the 18 months when he lived among them and taught them the new traditions of the New Covenant in A.D. 50-51.

How do we know I Corinthians 14:34-35 is a quotation of what the Jews believed about women being silent in the assembly and not what Paul believed? And how do we know the very next two verses I Corinthians 14:36-57 are a powerful refutation from Paul regarding this tradition? There are at least five solid hermeneutical reasons for holding to this view.

1. As already mentioned, the two verses that contain the quotation of what the Jews believed about women (I Corinthians 14:34-35) are completely antithetical to everything Paul writes about women throughout the New Testament, especially his teaching regarding women in the rest of I Corinthians. These two verses (vs. 34-35) are jarring because they represent a position that Paul has already torn apart in his previous writings.

2. The quotation of the Jews' belief in verses 34-35 is extremely consistent with the Law of God in the Jewish practices and Hebrew traditions (e.g. "The Law"). The Jews in Corinth accused Paul of persuading people "to worship God contrary to the Law" (Acts 18:13). If women being silent in the assembly actually represented Paul's beliefs, the Corinthian Jews would have hugged and kissed Sosthenes and Paul, not dragged them before the bema in Corinth in order to imprison them and/or beat them.

3. Paul wrote his first letter to the Corinthians in Greek. The written Greek language does not use "italics" as we do in our English to identify a quotation. To know being written something is a quotation:

a. The author must identify that what he is writing is a quotation (something Paul does elsewhere), or

b. The quotation must be so familiar to the audience that no identification of the quote is necessary, or

c. The author uses a Greek eta after the quotation to then refute it.

I believe both b. and c. are precisely how the Apostle Paul identifies he is quoting someone else in I Corinthians 14:34-35.

4). The Jews in Corinth, like all orthodox Jews in Paul's day, believed women were not qualified to be learners in the synagogue, and especially serve as teachers, because the Law and the Talmudic literature forbade them from learning. A woman's presence in the synagogue was tolerated, but women were to be unobtrusive and silent, never interfering with the work of the men. The Jews believed when a woman desired to ask a question in order to learn, she was to maintain her silence in the assembly and wait to ask her husband after leaving the synagogue and returning home.

The Jews believed the husbands were to be the source of their wives' learning. The Corinthian Jews were "zealous for the Law" and constantly opposed Paul's promotion of women as equal to men, including Priscilla and Aquila, the couple with whom Paul stayed in Corinth and who both later teach Apollo "the way of God more accurately" in Ephesus (see Acts 18:26). The quotation in I Corinthians 14:34-35 is consistent with the law of the Jews in Corinth, but it is absolutely contrary to the teaching and the practice of the Apostle Paul and the New Way of worship.

5). Paul REFUTES the Jewish quotation in I Corinthians 14:34-35 twice in the very next verse (v. 36) by using the Greek letter eta. Go look in your interlinear Greek/English Bible and find the stand alone Greek letter eta in v. 36. You will see the eta twice in that verse. It looks like this: η

The Greek eta has two possible markings that cause it to be translated with either the English word "or," or with the English equivalent of what we mean when we make a sound with our mouths like "PFFFFFFFFFFFFT!" This means "That's ridiculous!" or "Are you kidding me?" or "Nonsense!" This latter meaning, in my opinion, is precisely what Paul is saying (twice) in I Corinthians 14:36. In response to the Jewish quotation he has just given I Corinthians 14:35-36 Paul writes a Greek eta to illicit a sound from the reader "PFFFFFFFFT!" which is best translated "Nonsense!"

The original Greek text has no markings, so the proper translation of η must be obtained by translators based on facts other than the markings of the Greek letter. I believe the context, the culture of Corinth, and the radical nature of New Covenant worship taught by Paul (and resisted by the Corinthian Jews zealous for the Law) demands the η be translated with a "PFFFFFFFFFFFFT!" instead of "or" (as is done in the NAS). Between the written evidence of Paul's exasperation with the Judaizers limiting the role of women, the same women Jesus came to set free, Paul derisively dismisses the Jewish practice by speaking to the Judaizers and making an appeal to the Christians:

"Do you believe the Word of God comes to you only? If anyone wishes to think himself a prophet or spiritual, let that person recognize that the things I HAVE WRITTEN TO YOU (not what the Jews zealous for the Law teach) are the Lord's (e.g. "the Lord Jesus Christ's) commandment." (I Corinthians 14:36-37)

So, after reviewing the important historical, contextual, and grammatical factors that help get to the heart of Paul's meaning in I Corinthians 14:33-37, and using PFFFFFFT to translate the η, let's give a translation that is consistent with the rest of I Corinthians, Jesus' teaching and the Apostles' writings, and the New Covenant way of worship which is totally different than Old Covenant worship:

"For God is not a God of confusion but of peace, as in all the ecclesia of the saints. (Would you like an example?) 'The women are to keep silent in the churches; for they are not permitted to

speak, but are to subject themselves, just as the Law also says. If women desire to learn anything, let them ask their own husbands at home; for it is improper for a woman to speak in the church' PFFFFFFT! *Such nonsense! Do you Jews who practice this believe the Word of God comes from you only?* PFFFFFFT! *Do you believe the Word of God comes to you only? If anyone wishes to think himself a prophet or spiritual, let that person recognize that the things I* HAVE WRITTEN TO YOU *(not what the Jews zealous for the Law are teaching) are the Lord's commandment."*

The Apostle Paul quotes the Pharisaical Jews in Corinth the same way he quoted the pagan poets when he was in Athens. In Paul's famous message on Mars Hill, he says:

"God is not far from each one of us; for in him we live and move and exist, as even some of your own poets have said, "For we His offspring." Being the children of God, we ought not to think that the Divine Nature is like gold or silver or stone, an image formed by the art and thought of man" (Acts 17:27-29).

Are you familiar with the pagan poet Paul quotes from as he addressed the Athenians? Probably not. His name was Disoemeia, and he was a native of Paul's hometown of Tarsus. He was a Greek poet the Athenians loved to quote. He was also a worshipper of Zeus. I give you Robert Browning's English translation of Cicero's Latin version of Disoemeia's ancient Greek poem Divine Signs from which Paul quotes.

"From Zeus we lead the strain; he whom mankind
Ne'er leave unhymned: of Zeus all public ways,
All haunts of men, are full; and full the sea,
And harbours; and of Zeus all stand in need.
For we are His offspring: and he, ever good and mild
Gives favouring signs, and rouses us to toil.
Calling to mind life's wants: when clods are best
For plough and mattock: when time is ripe
For planting vines and sowing seeds, he tells
Since he himself hath fixed in heaven these signs."

Paul quotes both pagan poets and proud Pharisees in Scripture, and if you use these quotations as if they are the Word of God, you will make the same mistakes that pagans and Pharisees make in their religious practices.

Just because you quote a passage from the Bible does not necessarily mean you are revealing the mind of God. Serious, Bible-believing Christians recognize that no individual verse or passage of Scripture can be correctly interpreted outside of the textual context and an understanding of the cultural climate of those to whom the letter was initially written.

The issue of women's' function and roles in the church generates much heat in the evangelical church.

Those of us who believe in the infallibility of the sacred text should be very careful before using one's views on this issue as the standard for Christian orthodoxy. There is at least the possibility, if I'm correct in my interpretation, that those who urge women to be silent in the church because they "believe what the Bible says" actually may have more in common in their positions with pagan poets and proud Pharisees than the teachings of the Apostle Paul and Christ Himself.

Let's be humble about our position on women and realize that those of us who believe the Bible is the infallible Word of God always should be careful to discover what the Bible means.

Chapter 11: Defining "Sin" in the New Covenant as an Absence of Faith, Hope and Love

I was listening online to a Southern Baptist preacher and seminary professor preaching at a metropolitan First Baptist Church. He spoke on reasons believers ought to *"abstain from sin."* I often multi-task listening to online preachers, but it was the manner in which the preacher said "sin" that caused me to cease all other activities and listen intently. Some preachers, such as this one, have the habit of turning the single syllable word "sin" into multi-syllables such as "si-un" or "si-in." *It seems the exaggeration of sin's pronunciation serves as their declaration of sin's abomination.*

Hearing "sin" dramatically pronounced is when I began to listen closely. "How," I thought, "would this preacher describe sin for his congregation?" I didn't have to wait long for an answer. Sin was described as 'viewing internet pornography, cursing someone who cut you off on the road, not obeying authority in your life,' and a "list" of other activities that gave the listener - at least me - the distinct impression that "sin" was something easily identified and measurable *in other people.* That's what lists do. Lists label to enable.

There's a big problem when it comes to "labeling" sin for the Christian. When I was a kid, sin was defined as "transgressing the Law of God." It was explained to me that "transgression" was to "cross the boundary," and that the Law of God was a boundary "not to be crossed." All well and good; except for the fact as a kid I was very confused with what God's Law was for me as a believer in Jesus Christ.

The Jews set down 613 Commandments in the Old Testament that were not to be crossed, and they call these Laws of God the Mitzvot. I knew better than to argue with people who can read the Old Testament in its original Hebrew. *These Laws were real.* The Sabbath Laws, the Festival Laws, the Dietary Laws, and all the Laws of God in the Old Covenant were to be kept. Blessings came for obedience and punishments came for disobedience.

However, as I grew in my faith in Jesus Christ, I came to understand that *"all the Law and the Prophets"* were beautiful shadows and pictures of the Person and work of Jesus Christ (Luke 24:27). I came to see that *"Jesus fulfilled the Law - every jot and tittle of it"* for me (Matthew 5:18).

Through Christ's *active obedience* to the Law in His life and through Christ's *passive obedience* to the Law in His death (dying in my place), *"I am justified"* (i.e. "treated by God just-as-if-I-never-sinned and just-as-if-I-fully-obeyed") through my *"faith in Jesus Christ"* (Romans 5:1). God takes my faith and *"credits it to me as righteousness"* (Romans 4:22).

When I look at the Law of God, I only see Jesus Christ. He fulfilled the Law and then "set it aside *for a New Agreement"* (Hebrews 8:13). That New Covenant in His blood is a promise that those who "kiss the Son" through faith have the full pleasure of God. The Law and its observance became obsolete and abandoned through the destruction of the Temple in AD 70. I rest in the fact that God's love for me is *freely and forever mine* through my faith in Jesus Christ.

Free from the Law—oh, happy condition!
Jesus hath bled, and there is remission;
Cursed by the law and bruised by the fall,
Christ hath redeemed us once for all.

So, with all that said, what is "sin" as a Christian? How do I "define it" or how do I "describe it." In my opinion, if we make *lists* as to what is sin is *for other people*, then we will always emphasize the things *we don't do as sin, and keep off the list the things we do*. For example, you rarely hear a message on the sin of "eating-too-much" or "speaking-too-much" or "thinking-too-much-of -yourself" because those are the things preachers do! But it's sure easy to speak against "homosexuality" and "adultery" and "gambling" and "drinking" because those are things that preachers don't do!

The problem is *the creation of a list.* The Law of Israel is gone - fulfilled in Christ. But for some reason churches create new lists of 613 "Christian Commandments" like "tithing" and "not running in the house of God" and "obeying the words of the preacher/God's prophet" and .... Well, you get the idea. The lists change according to the denomination and the preacher-in-charge (like the one to whom I was listening), but the lists are there. That's the problem.

I propose that as a New Covenant believer in Jesus Christ, I may frame my understanding and description of "sin" around the things which "abide" or "continue on" in the New Covenant era (i.e. "this side of the cross.") Those three things which abide in this age are *"faith, hope and love, but the greatest of these is love"* (I Corinthians 13:13)

Faith

"Whatever is not of faith is sin," says the Apostle Paul (Romans 14:23b). If I think that by my activity I earn the favor and blessings of God (i.e. *eating meat offered to idols/or not eating meat offered to idols*), then I am "sinning" due to my lack of faith! Faith leads me to believe that God's favor rests on me because of my trust in *"the righteousness of His Son"* and not because of my obedience to "any Law" (Philippians 3:9). *Whatever is not of faith that the blessings of God are secured for you through the obedience of Jesus Christ is sin.*

Hope

"We give thanks for the faith and love that spring from *the hope stored up for you in heaven* and about which you have already heard in the true message of the gospel" (Colossians 1:5). The hope of these believers in Colossae was *everlasting happiness because of the inheritance reserved for them as co-heirs with Jesus Christ* (see Titus 2:13 and Galatians 5:5). This is why they kept "their minds on things above, and not on the things of this earth" (Colossians 3:2). This inheritance, which all believers receive by faith in Jesus Christ, is called "the object of our hope" because it is not yet possessed. Receiving the rewards Christ earned - *as a co-heir with Him* (Romans 8:17) - is future. *Whatever in this life causes you to lose sight of this hope stored up for you in heaven is sin.*

Love

"But the greatest of these is love" (I Corinthians 13:13). For "by this love will all know that you are My disciples" (John 13:35). The Royal Law of the New Covenant—the greatest Commandment given by the New Lawgiver (Jesus Christ)—is so clear it cannot be misunderstood. "A new commandment I give to you, that you love one another even as I have loved you" (John 13:34). Jesus loved me selflessly, sacrificially, and unconditionally. *To whatever extent I don't love others as Jesus has loved me, then I sin.*

Conclusion: Rather than making "a list" of sin for other people, maybe we'd be better off by examining our own lives for sin, and defining and describing sin for us as *"a lack of faith in Christ's love for me, a lack of hope in His promises to me, and my lack of love for others because I'm not resting my faith and my hope in Christ.*

Chapter 12: We Give as Led by the Spirit in the New Covenant Rather than the Law of the Tithe

Today there is an ongoing discussion by preachers and laymen regarding the practice of teaching what is called "storehouse tithing." The discussion is a good one, the only negative being the tendency of some to personalize disagreement by making moral judgments against those who view things differently than they do. Some who believe in "storehouse tithing" have called those who don't "antinomian" (meaning people who are "against God's Law"), and some who don't believe in storehouse tithing have a tendency to call those preachers who do "greedy" or "selfish." My name and church have been brought into the discussion, so I thought I would take this opportunity to share my beliefs on the matter.

I do not believe "storehouse tithing" is a biblical, New Covenant law or doctrine. But I respect those who do. The hermeneutic or interpretative principle that leads me to reject any "law" for how and where New Covenant Christians should give their money comes from the mountain (Mount Tabor). Mount Tabor is the traditional mountain where Jesus was transfigured--where He changed in appearance--before Peter, James and John (Mark 9:2-9). Mark writes that when the disciples saw Jesus transformed, they became very afraid. Their fear was heightened when they saw the Lawgiver of Israel (Moses) and the prophet of Israel (Elijah) suddenly standing next to Jesus and conversing with Him. Peter, not knowing what to do or say, blurts out, "Teacher, it is good that we all are here. Let us make three tents: One for You, and one for Moses, and one for Elijah." (v.5).

Suddenly, a cloud descended and a Voice spoke to the disciples, "This is my beloved Son; listen to Him!" When the cloud disappeared the disciples looked around and saw NOBODY BUT JESUS.

The original two words that form the last sentence in God's instructions to the disciples are *"akoute auton"* - Hear Him! Christ's voice is the voice to which we listen. He supersedes the Old Covenant Law of Moses and the Old Covenant sayings of the prophets. Hear Him! The Old Covenant ceremonial, civil, festival, dietary, and moral laws portray the Person and work of Christ for us. Likewise, the Old Covenant prophets portrayed through their ministry and words some aspect of the Person and work of the everlasting Prophet, Priest and King—Jesus Christ.

But the Old Covenant, in the days of the disciples, possessed a "fading glory" (II Corinthians 3:13). The New Covenant, signed and sealed by the blood of Christ, is far superior in nature and glory! Whereas in the Old Covenant, you reaped the rewards of your personal obedience to the law, in the New Covenant, you reap the rewards of His personal obedience in your place. As Paul says, "I have a righteousness of my own that does not come from my obedience to any law, but a righteousness that comes from God and is mine through faith" (Philippians 3:9). Having my hope and confidence in Christ, I listen to Him! He is my Master. I "akoute auton." I hear Him!

There is, however, a slight problem. Unlike the disciples that walked with Christ on earth, we can't see Christ visibly or hear Him audibly. We can't physically walk with Him, personally and audibly talk with Him, privately eat with Him, or publicly minister with Him—so how in the world do we "hear Him" since He's gone? Jesus answers this question. Right before He left the disciples to "Go and prepare a place for those who love Him," He said something astonishing. "It is to your advantage that I go away, for if I do not go away, the Helper will not come to you. But if I go, I will send Him to you . . . When the Spirit of truth comes, the Spirit will guide you. . ." (John 16:7-8, 13).

It's interesting to note that the 2000 Baptist Faith and Message, the confession of faith of Southern Baptists, makes a pronounced error when it comes to the Spirit of God. In Article II C, on 'God the Holy Spirit,' the 2000 Baptist Faith and Message states, "At the moment of regeneration the Holy Spirit baptizes every believer into the Body of Christ." That's just not right. Nowhere in the Bible does it ever say the Spirit baptizes anybody. Christ baptizes us in the Spirit.

It might be a shock to some of our brethren to learn the *BFM 2000* is not inerrant. John the Baptist said "*Jesus will baptize you with* [lit., "in", the Gk. Preposition en] *the Holy Spirit and with fire*" (Matthew 3:11; Mark 1:8; Luke 3:16; John 1:33; Acts 1:5; 11:16). Why does Jesus immerse us completely in His Spirit? Because the Holy Spirit is His gift to us; He is "another" (Gk. alloy - "of the same kind") Comforter who leads Christ's disciples. In other words, in as simple language as possible, the disciples were instructed by God to hear Christ.

But Christ ascended into heaven, so He now baptizes all those who trust Him in the Holy Spirit. Hear Him! Hear the Spirit! We are called by God to "walk by the Spirit," to "listen to the Spirit," as we serve, give, witness, etc... The royal law of Christ is to love one another as He has loved us, but the way we practically live out that commandment is to "listen to the Spirit of God" as He guides us while we live in this world.

Simply put, in the New Covenant agreement with God, you *listen to the Spirit as to how you are to invest your money in His Kingdom*. There is no law. There is no code. There is the Spirit. Hear Him. And, by the way, the Spirit of God leading His people brings about powerful, even miraculous, things in this world. Those who obey the Spirit aren't antinomian at all—they are Spirit led.

Probably the clearest writing I've read on this subject as it pertains to Christian giving is an article written by, of all people, Dr. John R. Rice. He writes:

"When anybody takes from a man the right to go to Jesus
Christ and get instructions and follow Him, he is on the
way to greater heresies. Popery of a Baptist preacher is
wrong just like popery of Rome is wrong. If a pastor has a
right to tell the people where their money must go, then a
local denominational secretary will have the right to say
so, too. If a church will have a right to tell you where you
can give your money, it will have a right to tell you what
you must believe also. If a church can tell you that you
have no right to inquire directly from God about where to
give your money, then the church can tell you that you
have no right to come to Christ for salvation except as you
come through the local church and let the church decide
it. That way is Catholicism and that is wrong. Any bold and
insistent step into heresy means further heresy ahead.
Giving? Oh, yes. Giving tithes and offerings? Oh, yes, and
far beyond that as I have delighted to do now for many,
many years. If God leads, give it all through the local
church, but only as He leads. But remember . . . (Jesus) has
a right to say where it should go. No one has a right to take
this crown right of Jesus Christ and put it on a preacher or
board of deacons or a finance committee."

I guess you could call what I believe about giving to the local
church "Mt. Tabor giving" instead of Mt. Sinai giving.

Akoute Auton! Listen to the Spirit of God as He leads you in the
amount you give, where He leads you to give it, and when He leads
you to give it. It's all the Lord's anyway. Hear Him!

As a pastor, I trust that the Spirit will supply the needs of our
church ministries through the promptings He gives people. If not,
we will change how we do ministry, seeking to follow His
leadership. He definitely does not need me to issue a law.

Chapter 13: Live by Faith in Christ and the New Covenant and Never "Draw Back"

Four times the Bible uses the phrase "The righteous will live by faith" (Habakkuk 2:4; Romans 1:17; Galatians 3:13; Hebrews 10:38). It's obvious that "faith" is important in the Bible. In fact, these four verses could be translated "By faith the righteous live."

Faith sustains the righteous as much as it saves the righteous. "Kiss the Son" - that is, embrace by faith the Son of God - and He will not be angry (Psalm 2:12). In Hebrews 10:38, the fourth passage where Scripture states "the righteous will live by faith," the writer of Hebrews goes on to say that God is not pleased with the one who "draws back" from faith.

"But My righteous one will live by faith. And I take no pleasure in the one who draws back" (Hebrews 10:38).

The terminology "draws back" is a phrase from the battlefield and references one who moves from a position of vulnerability to a fortress in a high place, seemingly protected. It is the same language used by the prophet Habakkuk when he describes "the proud one, the one whose soul is not right within him." He is the one who "draws back to the high places" (Hebrews 10:38), but "the righteous live by faith" (Habakkuk 2:4).

The great 12th century Hebrew linguist, R. Moses Kimchi, comments on Habakkuk 2:4 and says, "He whose soul is not right in him places himself in a fortress or tower, to set himself on high there from the enemy, and does not return to God, nor seek deliverance of Him; but the righteous has no need to place himself on high in a fortress, for he lives by his faith. "

John Gill agrees that the proud one is he whose "soul is not right" and "places himself in a fortress or tower," drawing back into what he deems his safe place. Gill, like R. Moses Kimchi, believes the words of Habakkuk refers to proud Jews,

"...who boast of their Temple, and glory in it, and trust in their service and sacrifices at it; and trust in themselves, their religious rites and ceremonies, the traditions of their elders, and their moral works of righteousness for their tower of safety and their place of defense; neglecting the Messiah, the Rock of salvation."

Gill points out that the Temples sat in a high place called Ophel, part of the mountain of Zion in Jerusalem, and it was to that place proud Jews ran for their comfort of right standing with God.

But by faith the righteous live.

I am often amazed at the number of people who understand that faith is important, but have very little understanding that the object of one's faith is primary in Scripture. Everyone has faith, but not everyone has faith in the Messiah. Some, like those Habakkuk calls "right in their souls," run to their religion, or to their commitment, or to their rituals, or to their traditions, or to their service, or to their self-righteousness -- their haughty and high mountain - for their place of defense and security.

But by faith the righteous live.

Those who are really righteous never draw away from faith in the Messiah's Person, work and obedience. Those who just place their faith in the Messiah's substitutionary death, burial and resurrection. The righteous trust in the Messiah's work, both His active and passive obedience, and never their own, whether it be their past or present commitments and promises.

But by faith the righteous live.

Quick. Write down twenty things for which you trust Christ. We should be able to give a thousand reasons for the "hope within us," but I'm only asking for twenty.

I trust Christ for_____

When you can quickly write down twenty things for which you trust Christ, you will begin to experience the joy and peace that comes from resting in the "better promises" of the New Covenant.

For it is by faith the righteous live.

Chapter 14: Regrets Have No Place in My Life under the New Covenant

The title of this chapter contains a strong sentence because it is opposite of the way most people, even Christians, live their lives. Most people think "Oh my, if I would have only ..." or "What a shame, if I could have just ..." or "I'm so sad because I should have ...".

Because of these thoughts, many people live lives full of regret. I want to show you from Scripture that there's no place for regretful thoughts in the life of a Christ-believer. Stuff happens; but God happens to be over our happenstances. In Romans 8:28 God promises to those who've embraced His Son that He will turn all things for good. This means even our mistakes, into ultimate good for His eternal glory. Let me show you a powerful example of this Romans 8:28 principle.

There's a verse in Acts 26:31 that many Christians pass quickly over without giving it serious thought. I'll quote the verse in just a moment, but let me set the context. Paul has been accused of blasphemy for bringing Gentiles into the Temple, a capital offense among the Jews. He stands trial before Felix in Caesarea on charges of inciting riots, being the leader of a sect of people who follow "the Nazarene," and of desecrating the Temple (see Acts 24:5-8).

Eventually King Agrippa, the Roman puppet king over the Jews, assists Felix during Paul's trial because Paul had appealed to Rome as a Roman citizen, being from the Roman city of Tarsus. Paul convincingly argues to both Felix and Agrippa that he is doing nothing contrary to the Jewish religion and that he "worships the God of our fathers" (Acts 24:14-15) and is innocent of all charges.

Both Felix and Agrippa believe Paul is innocent of blasphemy charges, but in Acts 26:31 Agrippa makes a stunning statement:

"This man could have been set free if he had not appealed to Caesar."

Ouch. Don't gloss over that statement lightly. Paul, in chains and in prison for two years, facing capital charges, could have been set free, if he had not...

Put yourself in Paul's shoes. What do you think he's thinking at that moment? Prison is not fun. Two years is a long time. This episode of arrest, two-year imprisonment, and ultimate trial in Caesarea occurred after Paul's third missionary journey. While Paul had been waiting for his hearing before Festus and Agrippa, there had not been many people to whom Paul could minister the gospel. Paul had known what it meant to be a success in Christ's Kingdom, but for two years he's been a prisoner in chains. Surely Paul wanted out of prison, right? Certainly Paul wanted to go on a fourth missionary trip, yes? If Paul is like us, he had to have believed being in prison was far worse than being out of prison. Wouldn't you? I think so.

Yet Paul hears, "You could have been set free if you had not...." At that moment, I'm sure the enemy launched the fiery darts of deep disappointment toward Paul. Regret had to have been assaulting the gate of Paul's heart. It's a little like you hearing, "You could have....if you had not...", or you thinking, "I should have...but I did not..." and all the feelings that come your way during those occasions of regret.

But let me remind you what happened next to Paul. He is sent to Rome and placed in custody there. While in prison he shares Christ with both his fellow inmates and officials from Caesar's court. He also writes letters that we know as the Prison Epistles— Ephesians, Colossians, Philemon, and Philippians. It's possible that the initial infiltration of the gospel into the Legion of Thunder and Caesar's court began with Paul's imprisonment in Rome. It is certain that all the encouragement we've received from the Prison Epistles can be traced to Paul's imprisonment in Rome.

More precisely, all the good that's come our way through reading Paul's epistles can be traced back to a day of potentially great disappointment for Paul.

He *coulda, woulda, shoulda* been free from prison after his second year, but he appealed to Rome. Again, I imagine Paul initially thought he had messed up. However, we learn from Paul's life the Romans 8:28 principle that God always has other plans for us, much better plans, even when we think we've screwed up big time.

Regret is a poison pill. It darkens the soul and deadens the senses. It's a fog that descends and clouds your surroundings, so that you have difficulty engaging what's in front of you, enjoying what's around you, and escaping what's behind you.

Regret has no place in the Christian life because our good Father turns around everything in our lives for our good. Everything. Everything includes our mistakes, our sins, our tragedies, our screw-ups, our "wrong" decisions, and everything else that leads us to "*coulda, shoulda, woulda*" thinking.

When your mind begins to be filled with regret, squash it and get rid of it like you do a roach found in your kitchen. It's an invader; it's an intruder in a space where it does not belong. God takes all of our *couldas, wouldas and shouldas* and works them for our ultimate good and His ultimate glory. That's the kind of Heavenly Father we have; He is all-powerful and always good.

Believe it and live it.

Chapter 15: The Scars of Law in the Old Covenant and the Riches of Grace in the New Covenant

"I have been the biggest hypocrite ever." Those were the first public words from Josh Duggar after hackers released information that Mr. Duggar spent hundreds of dollars at Ashley Madison, a website designed for married people who desire to have extra-marital sexual affairs.

Mr. Duggar, the former Vice-President of the Family Research Council, had worked tirelessly in opposition to gay marriage, internet pornography, and other moral and social issues. All the while, Mr. Duggar lived a secret life of "pornography addiction...and marital infidelity." The public exposure of Mr. Duggar's duplicity - or to use his word, hypocrisy - has set Twitter and social media on fire.

Hackers released the email addresses and credit card usage of 32 million users of Ashley Madison - but the media is focusing like a laser beam on Josh Duggar. Why is there a media and cultural infatuation with a twenty-seven-year-old Christian whose singular claim to fame is being the eldest son of a family featured on a second-rate reality television show?

The Advocate, an online news organization promoting gay, lesbian and transgender lifestyles writes that the Duggars have "a long history of anti-LGBT" rhetoric and actions. The Duggars have promoted "family values" and have called homosexuality a sin. It seems that *The Advocate* and other media have the rationale that, "if readers can see the lies and hypocrisy of Josh Duggar's life, then surely they'll understand the lies and deception of Josh Duggar's words."

That's why Josh Duggar has been singled out among 32 million Ashley Madison users. Those who don't like the idea that moral law actually comes from our Creator will seize on anything to convince themselves and others that there is actually no moral law from God. Promoting hypocrisy in the life of one who speaks freely of Divine Law makes those who despise the concept of moral law feel better about the possibility that God's Law doesn't even exist. It's not news when an atheist has an affair.

However, those who have singled out Josh Duggar from among the 32 million Ashley Madison users are probably ignorant of the fact that God's Law was only designed to expose the problem within us and never designed to expunge the problem from us. I'm an evangelical preacher of the gospel. I'm not surprised by any moral failure in the life of any Christian who publicly and repeatedly promotes God's Laws to the world. Not only am I not surprised; I expect it. No matter how boldly one proclaims that adultery and homosexuality are violations of God's moral law, Divine law has no power to remove desires for adultery or homosexuality from within our hearts.

God's Law Changes Nobody, It Only Scars

God declares adultery to be a violation of His moral standard. "You shall not commit adultery," God says (Exodus 20:14). Solomon wrote, "The person who commits adultery has no sense; whoever does it destroys his or her own life" (Proverbs 6:32). Likewise, God calls homosexuality "an abomination," a violation of His intention for the world (Leviticus 18:22). Paul says those who commit homosexuality have *"taken the truth of God and exchanged it for a lie, worshiping and serving created things rather than the Creator"* (Romans 1:25).

God's Law was given to expose corruption in the heart and to restrain actions by the sinner; but it was never designed to expunge corruption from the heart or to reverse actions by the sinner. The Law is powerless to change us.

But we know that the Law is good, if one uses it the way it was intended, realizing the fact that law is not made for a righteous person, but for those who are lawless and rebellious, for the ungodly and sinners, for the unholy and profane, for those who kill their fathers or mothers, for murderers and immoral men and homosexuals and kidnappers and liars and perjurers, and whatever else is contrary to sound teaching" (1 Timothy 1:8–11).

The Law scars. It might restrain, but the person restrained by law is scarred by the battle to throw it off. Sadness, unhappiness, despair, depression and all other emotions that bubble up when being held or restrained from obtaining the very thing the heart wants will lead the sinner to fight against God's restraints (the law). Let me illustrate this principle.

Odysseus, the great captain of the seas in ancient Greece, knew that the island of the Sirens was an island to be avoided. The beautiful half-naked, woman-like creatures who inhabited the island would sing their beautiful songs to entice sailors to enter their port. The Sirens would then attack the sailors, maiming and killing them before consuming their bodies.

To avoid this sensuous but deadly island, Odysseus ordered his men to bind him with ropes, to put wax in their own ears, and then ordered the sailors to tighten the ropes when they saw their captain fighting against them. As Odysseus and his men sailed by the island of the Sirens, Odysseus heard the beautiful music and wanted with all his might to swim to the Sirens. He fought against the ropes. The sailors, with wax in their ears, tightened the ropes. Odysseus fought harder. He would later say,

"I became desperate to plunge into the sea."

The sailors used the ropes to restrain Odysseus, and the ship eventually sailed by the island of the Sirens, avoiding certain destruction and death of Odysseus and his men. But Odysseus was scarred for life. The ropes couldn't change his desires; they only prevented him from obtaining them. The legacy of Odysseus fighting against the restraints could be seen in the physical scars he bore.

God's Law is like the ropes that constrained Odysseus. It may be used to bind others, as a civil society may choose restraints in the form of laws that prohibit adultery and homosexuality (as America once did), but those others will fight against those laws until they are thrown off, because the Law cannot change the heart.

This is why it should never be surprising to any of us when those who advocate tightening the ropes wind up falling into the sea themselves.

God's Riches in Christ Is Beautiful Music Indeed

So how do we actually change? How do we avoid the Ashley Madison websites of this world? How do we say no to our addictions? How do we sail by the island of the Sirens? What has the power to change us?

According to the New Testament, the only thing powerful enough to change us from the inside/out is the riches of God's grace toward us in Jesus Christ. It's never the Law of God that convinces a man to change his life; it's the grace and goodness of God in Christ that has the power to change the human heart.

We must become captivated by a sweeter, more beautiful song.

Going back to Greek mythology, Jason was another captain who sailed the Aegean Sea. He and his men, the Argonauts, had also heard that the island of the Sirens was beautiful but deadly. Unlike Odysseus, Jason didn't sail by the island bound by ropes and with wax in his men's ears. Jason asked Orpheus, the greatest musician in the world, to sail with him and his men.

When they came near to the island of the Sirens, Orpheus began playing his music. Jason and his men were so captivated by what they heard from Orpheus that when the Sirens began singing their songs, they sailed right on by because their hearts were captured by more beautiful music.

This is what the message of God's grace in Jesus Christ does for us. It's a sweeter song. The problem is that many who name Christ as Lord often seemed more concerned with tightening the ropes than creating beautiful music.

Yesterday I performed a funeral service for an elderly woman who died of Alzheimer's disease. I chose as my text God's incredible promise to those who trust His Son: "I will remember your sins and iniquities no more" (Hebrews 8:12). I explained that God's forgetfulness, unlike Alzheimer's, is intentional, personal, and eternal.

When you begin to live in the knowledge of God's forgetfulness of all those times you "missed the mark" (sin) as a spouse, person, parent, etc... then you can relate to God not out of fear nor "obedience to any law," but in the knowledge of His great grace for you in Jesus Christ. After the message, a couple unfamiliar with true Christianity, told me that the message had "changed their lives." God's grace is the only thing powerful enough to change lives.

A life lived to its fullest comes from listening to the beautiful music that is struck by the chords of God's riches in Christ. Even when we screw up intentionally and wickedly (i.e. "iniquity"), God forgets it because Jesus died for it.

That's rich grace; and it alone will change our hearts. The music of grace causes us to lose the desire for the lesser pleasures of sin and iniquity. Our lives change when we begin to feel that God's grace for us is more beautiful, more pleasurable, more captivating, and more enticing than our sin.

When I come to realize that I can jump into the sea and He'll never hold it against me, and when I come to understand that if I jump for a lesser pleasure I'm acting senselessly by abandoning my only real Treasure, and when I find myself swimming to a lesser pleasure that will ultimately only destroy me, then maybe it's time for me to ask why I'm not being captivated by the beautiful music of God's grace in Jesus Christ?

If, however, I hear the beautiful music of grace, and if I begin to walk in the deep and unconditional love of God for me, then I indeed discover that I need no illicit love to fill my heart. And if I come to revel in the sweetness of God's intentional and personal forgiveness of me, then I find the power to throw off any addiction that helped me deal with the pain and guilt of my failures.

And if I come to understand that God, who spared not His Own Son for me, will freely, daily and cheerfully give me everything I need, then I will be unable to find any reason to spend time worrying about tomorrow.

I have Him.

The Beautiful Music of God's Grace in Christ Changes the Heart

Ephesians 2:7 ... *"God sent His Son so "that in the ages to come He might show the surpassing riches of His grace in kindness toward us in Christ Jesus."*

Romans 9:23... *"God gave us His Son "make known the riches of His glory upon vessels of mercy..."*

Ephesians 1:7... *"In Him we have redemption through His blood, the forgiveness of our trespasses, according to the riches of His grace."*

I Timothy 1:14... *"And the grace of our Lord was more than abundant, with the faith and love which are found in Christ Jesus."*

John 10:10...Jesus said, *"The thief comes only to steal and kill and destroy; I have come that you may have life, and that you might have life at its fullest."*

If you've understood what I've written above, you understand my life's message. I'm not sure if it's clear to you or not, but after reading about Josh Duggar this morning, I felt compelled to write for those Duggars out there not yet caught.

Real change comes from rich grace.

Chapter 16: Decision Making and Mutual Submission in Marriage Under the New Covenant

The attitude of every follower of Jesus Christ, whether male or female, is one of servant-like submission. "Do nothing from selfishness or empty conceit, but with humility of mind regard one another as more important than yourselves" (Philippians 2:3). *"Have this attitude in yourselves which was also in Christ Jesus, who.... took the form of a bond-servant"* (Philippians 2:5-7).

The best one-word description for this servant-like attitude of "regarding another as more important" is the word submission. To be a submissive person is to be like the bond-slave Jesus Christ became for us. The Bible is emphatic that all Christians, both males and females, are to be characterized by love and submission to other people.

Paul describes this Spirit-filled life of believers in Ephesians 5 where he writes, "and walk in love, just as Christ also has loved you..." (v. 2). Then later in the same chapter Paul writes, "And be submissive to one another" (v. 21). Again, these two characteristics of the Spirit-filled life (love and submission) are mandatory regardless of gender. Paul illustrates how love and submission work in the husband/wife relationship in the rest of chapter 5.

"Wives to your own husbands" (v. 22) is what Paul literally writes. Unfortunately, English translators add the words "be subject" after the word wives. Why do our English translators leave off "love?" In other words, why didn't they say, "and wives be submissive to and

loving to your husbands"? Paul is writing about love AND submission. When he writes "wives to your husbands" the emphasis should always be "Wives, be submissive and loving to your husbands."

Likewise, Paul writes "so husbands to wives" (v. 28). Again, the English translation picks up on the word "love" for husbands the word "love" is not in the original Greek in verse 28. In the context of mutual love and mutual submission (v. 2 and v. 21), husbands are to express a love and a servant-like spirit of submission to their wives. It may sound strange to your ears to hear that the Bible says a husband is to be submissive to his wife, but it wasn't strange to Paul's ears. This is the teaching of the New Covenant. To say that a husband is to have a submissive attitude toward his wife and love her as Christ loves him is as correct as saying that a wife is to love her husband and be submissive to him. No gender, whether male or female, is to leave off either submission or love in human relationships.

Because the Scripture teaches mutual servant-like submission and unconditional love for both the husband and the wife, some Christians who are unfamiliar with Scripture—but who have been indoctrinated with institutional church dogmatism about "authority" – may be confused. "How will a married couple ever make a decision if nobody is the boss and everybody has an attitude of servant-like submission and unconditional love?" they might ask.

Great question. Here is how a Spirit-filled couple makes a decision in marriage.

1. *Both the husband and wife are able to freely give their opinions and express disagreement because* the husband considers his wife "more important" than himself and the wife views her husband "more important" than herself, so each desires to hear what the other person has to say.

2. *The husband listens to his wife and the wife listens to her husband* because there are reciprocal love and respect for one

another. This love and respect is the same kind of love and respect that the husband and wife have both experienced from Jesus Christ. If one objects by saying, "But how does submit to the His bride?" Answer: He died for us. He serves us both now and in heaven.

3. *If unity of desire and mutual agreement for the proper course of action cannot be found, then the couple mutually agrees to wait on making a decision.* They that wait upon the Lord shall be renewed in strength. During this time of waiting, the husband asks God for wisdom and discernment for himself, and the wife asks God for wisdom and discernment for herself.

4). *After waiting, when the deadline for a decision approaches, the husband--in a spirit of love and submission toward his wife—will either be led by the Holy Spirit to begin having the same desires as his wife, OR, the wife—in a spirit of love and submission toward her husband will be led by the Holy Spirit to begin having the same desires as her husband.* Two Christians living together are to honor God by living in harmony with one another. That's not to say that the husband and wife are to be the same; harmony recognizes the beauty of differences, and incorporates those differences into a beautiful melody. Mutual submission is the art of hearing from God.

5). *In a Christ-honoring marriage, no person sees himself (or herself) as the "authority" in the home.* Jesus Christ has "all authority" (Matthew 28:18), and a marriage that honors God is one where both the husband and the wife look to Christ alone as their authority. Decision making is made with a spirit of mutual submission and love, leaning on Christ to produce unity of hearts and minds.

For anyone married to an unbeliever, this process of coming to unity in decision making may be a tad harder. This is why the New Covenant writers issue a caution about being unequally yoked. However, when two followers of Jesus Christ are married, it is important to remember that Scripture clearly teaches submission is never the wife's responsibility to the exclusion of the husband's, nor is love the responsibility of the husband's to the exclusion of the wife's. A Spirit-filled, Christ-honoring, God-glorifying marriage is one of mutual submission and love.

Chapter 17: The New Covenant: The Extraordinary Beauty of Loving Without Needing

I will often begin a talk with husbands or wives at various marriage conferences with the statement, "The best marriages are those where a husband and wife love each other, but don't need each other." Most of the time after saying this, couples look at me with a "deer-in-the-headlights" expression. I can see the wheels turning as they try to grasp what's been said. Usually speakers at marriage conferences say the opposite.

The typical marriage speaker will tell wives that they are to expect their basic human needs to be met by their husband, and husbands that they should expect their wives to meet their basic needs. Then a list of the wife's needs is given to the husband, and a list of the husband's needs is given to the wife. Couples often leave average marriage conferences with both huge expectations and even greater burdens to do for their mate what God never designed us to do, to be the source of one's identity through the meeting of each other's spiritual, psychological, emotional and physical needs.

I can prove from Scripture that God never designed a spouse to be the person on whom one depends for basic needs. At first, such a concept might seem strange. But follow the logic. We innately know, and the Bible affirms, that the basic needs of all human beings, both men and women, are as follows:

1. The need to connect with others (love or social belonging),

2. The need for respect (significance), and

3. The need to protect (security).

God designed us to have these basic needs met by Him, not our spouses. My basic needs are to be met by union with Christ, not the union I have with my mate. Let me prove it:

"My God shall supply all your needs according to His riches in glory" (Philippians 4:19).

It is not "your husband" (or "your wife") who shall supply all your needs. The Bible reveals that Jesus gave much practical comfort to His disciples, both men and women (see Luke 8:1-3). Christ explicitly said that those who receive Him as Savior and Lord are not to worry about their future. He, their King, has everything under His control. He, not your spouse, will provide for all your needs. See Matthew 6:25-34 as an example of Christ's teaching on this subject. Any spouse who looks to a mate to provide basic needs is substituting that mate for Christ.

"At the resurrection, people will neither marry nor be given in marriage" (Matthew 22:30).

These are the words of Jesus. The resurrection is that time when God raises believers in Christ from the dead to live forever on the earth where the curse has been reversed. This is what Jesus meant when He said, "The meek will inherit the earth" (Matthew 5:5). When the redeemed earth is given to us as an inheritance, the city that Christ has been preparing for His people (see John 14:1-4, Hebrews 11:10, and Revelation 20) will descend from heaven and unite with this redeemed earth. This is the day that "all of creation is groaning for" (Romans 8:22).

Note to wives: Contrary to what Muslims, Mormons and other radical patriarchal advocates say, no woman will ever have her identity associated with a man for eternity.

Jesus will give each of us "a new name" (see Revelation 2:17). Names in Scripture represent a "change in identity or character." In heaven, you will "unfold the riches of His grace" and see all that He has prepared for you. Your worth, significance, identity and value will be found in Him. In your marriage here and now, you are to reflect your growing understanding of who you are in Christ as you love your mate the way Christ loves you. Jesus doesn't need you, but He sure does love you.

Any religion on this earth that refuses to assist women to find their basic needs met in Jesus Christ, any religion that refrains from pointing women to the King of Kings and encouraging them to revel in the riches of being "wed to Christ," and any religion that somehow tries to make a woman think she needs her husband (spiritually, emotionally, or materially) is a religion that is not based on the infallible Scriptures or the truth of God's Kingdom. On the other hand, those Christian women who have been set free from the bondage of believing that they need their husbands to meet their basic needs, and then simply love their husbands from the overflow of resting in the love and provisions of Christ, will find a slice of heaven in their homes.

"What causes quarrels and fightings among you? Don't they come from a battle over desires within you? You want something but don't get it. You quarrel and fight. You do not have, because you do not ask God" (James 4:1-2).

Angry quarrels, scornful fights, and other efforts to control and manipulate your spouse arise from a desire to have your basic needs met by your mate rather than by your God. God never designed your husband to take His place in your life. Christ alone is your Source of real and lasting love, personal and abiding significance, and unqualified daily security.

"Seek first the Kingdom of God," Jesus said. The Kingdom of God is best defined as God's reign in your life through Jesus Christ. His Kingdom is within you (Luke 17:21). One day His Kingdom will be all around you, but until then, His reign is within. For this reason, you don't need your husband to be a certain way. You may want certain things from your husband, and of course, there is nothing wrong with asking; but you don't need him to be a certain way. Why? Because every need you have is designed to be met by God.

Questions

"Why does the Bible speak of a man and a woman becoming 'one flesh' in marriage if marriage is not designed to be permanent and marriage is not the place that a man or woman is to receive his or her identity?"

Answer: Marriage is a picture of the union that a man and a woman individually have with Christ. One should never replace the reality with the picture. When you embrace and kiss the picture to the exclusion of what the picture represents, you become an unhealthy Christian.

Again, the example I've used before is picking up my wife up from the airport after a long absence, running toward her to greet her, and then suddenly stopping, ignoring my wife, and then pulling out a picture of her and kissing the picture. That's an unhealthy action. I have made an idol of the picture and missed the reality of what the picture represents.

Marriage is only a picture of the union you have with Christ. You are to get your identity from Christ, not your marriage.

Pictures and picture frames break. They rip, burn, fade, and are often destroyed. So, too, marriages break and fall apart, but they are only pictures of the reality of one's union with Christ. If the picture is destroyed, it never means the reality conveyed by the picture is gone. A spouse is to get his or her significance, security, and love from a union with Jesus Christ, and never a union with any man.

"What happens when my spouse breaks the vow of sexual fidelity or becomes emotionally or physically abusive to me?"

Answer: To say that a spouse's infidelity doesn't hurt would be false, thus all married persons want their spouse to be faithful.

However, to say I don't need a faithful mate is true. To say that a spouse's emotional and physical abuse doesn't hurt would be false. To say that I don't need my spouse to be kind, loving and gracious is true. A married person doesn't need to be married. I may want to be married, but I don't need to be married.

Therefore, if your spouse is unfaithful or abusive, confront your husband in love and draw a boundary. Tell your husband that you cannot control his actions, nor is it your desire to control him. Let him know that if he desires another woman, or if he feels the need to abuse you, then you will let him go. You can and will end the marriage because you do not need him. End it, however, not in spite, or anger, or manipulation or control. End the marriage because you refuse to enable your husband in his sin, or be a wife that remains in abuse because you can't live without your man. You can.

And, when the marriage is over, treat your former husband with dignity, respect and kindness--the same way you would treat any man who is not your husband, for that is the kind of person a woman who has her needs met in Christ is. Of course, the Spirit may lead you to stay with an adulterous spouse as He did Hosea to stay with Gomer, but it was not for Hosea's sake that he remained committed to an adulterous wife, it was for his wife's sake.

In some marriages, spouses will unintentionally enable their mates to continue in their addictions or sin because they unintentionally substitute their spouses for Christ. When a married person cannot envision a future without their spouse, then the picture (marriage) has become an idol, and the married person has lost perspective on the reality that marriage is intended to represent (my union with Christ).

"Can you be specific on the reasons my spouse may even be more attracted to me when I love my spouse without needing my spouse?"

Answer: Christ's love for us is magnetic. "We love Him because He first loved us" (I John 4:19). Christ does not need us. He doesn't need us to be happy. He doesn't need us to be fulfilled. He doesn't need us to be a certain way for Him to feel significant. When He loves us, it is a selfless love. His love is unconditional, and wells within Him like an artesian spring. We don't pull it out of Him; He loves because He is love. When we begin to understand and experience this unconditional and personal love, we are drawn toward Him.

In the same manner, when a fulfilled, self-sufficient person marries, that person doesn't need marriage. The Kingdom of God is God's total answer for man's total need. What a person needs is Christ. We are wed to Him, and our desires in marriage are to be all that Christ has made us in life.

Selfless love is magnetic. It draws a spouse. Granted, your mate may not at first understand selfless love, mainly because His needs are not yet being fully met by Christ via faith! For this reason, a spouse may become unfaithful by searching for fulfillment in others. A Christian must set boundaries in marriage, but the enforcement of those boundaries should always be done with dignity, respect and love for the unfaithful spouse – for the good of the one unfaithful.

There is an extraordinary beauty in loving without needing.

Chapter 18: Worship as a Way of Life Rather than a Rule of Law in the New Covenant

My father, Paul Burleson, who lives consistently by New Covenant principles writes some words of encouragement on worship in the New Covenant.

"I'M THINKING - There is not A SINGLE verse in the New Testament that even hints that the PURPOSE of the gathering of the church is for worship. The New Testament text shows that the purpose of the gathering is all of the "One Another" verses. In other words, it is for the horizontal relationships [plural] and NOT the vertical relationship [singular] that the Church gathers on any given occasion. I'm NOT saying to worship as a gathered congregation is WRONG. I'm just saying it is NOT the PRIMARY purpose for the gathered Body of Christ in the New Testament. I think that's where we are to be today as well.

John Piper said this, *"The very epistles that are written to help the church be what it ought to be in this age [are] almost totally devoid of...explicit teaching on the specifics of corporate worship"* There are some things that I disagree with John Piper about theologically, but NOT this.

I'M THINKING - Many churches today may be reflecting an "Old Covenant" way of thinking about worship rather than a "New Covenant" way of thinking? To "go to" a place and "to do" certain things a certain way, misses the boat on worship entirely as seen in the New Testament. In the Old Testament people DID COME to the Tabernacle/Temple [House of God] to meet with and worship Jehovah a certain way. They did bring such things such as sacrifices and offerings all the while performing their rituals regularly that led eventually to the High Priest entering into His Presence in the Tabernacle or Temple on that one occasion called the Day of Atonement.

But to see the Church in the New Testament trying to gather IN THAT WAY would be missing the point of the CROSS. Jesus Christ IS HIMSELF our sacrifice, our offering, our feast days, our cleansing, our sanctification, and all the rest that's pictured in the Old Testament Tabernacle OR Temple. Jesus IS our very life! We live DAILY in the presence of God and are to worship DAILY the One Who indwells us by His Holy Spirit. Worship for us is a life of obedience as we're recognizing His presence and enjoying HIM as being our source for All OF LIFE. Then there is a gathering occasionally to encourage and provoke one another. [See Romans 12:1-2 and Hebrews 10:25]

I'M THINKING - A debate about "music in worship" is a bit silly, if not totally futile. From" no instruments" on one side of the argument [Church of Christ], to those who enjoy what SOME MIGHT CALL "entertainment," [Lights and Sound, drums and guitars, such as we have in my church called HHBC]] there is a raging debate going on about it all. But my question is WHY does the way someone musically worships matter to us AT ALL?

In the New Testament music itself is simply NOT addressed, except being seen as a result of the Holy Spirit doing His infilling work. But things like washing feet, serving in love, sharing the Lord's table, teaching the saints and praying for others are addressed as a congregation. We call them the "one another" verses mentioned in the first paragraph. Even were one to hold to the Old Testament as an example of worship, [I don't, as you can tell] it needs to be remembered that the Israelites many times used drums, trumpet blasts, silence, repetitions, singing, shouting, and numerous other interesting displays to glorify God. Nothing calm, cool or collected about that.

I'M THINKING - Jesus REALLY DID mean something special when He announced that the day has come when those who worship will do so in Spirit and Truth? NO LONGER is worship to be based on doing it a certain way, a certain time or at a certain place. Nor is it supposed to be based on one generation's "form" of musical worship compared to another. IT IS A WAY OF LIFE!

So, as I read someone say and I paraphrase, whether in a room alone, or with others shouting and jumping with joy, or sitting in silence, or clapping to an electronic synthesizer, or with an organ or piano singing hymns, or just being intoxicated by his love as the Song of Solomon describes it, or even further, when we are reading aloud the Word, or feeding the poor, proclaiming the Good News to the broken-hearted in His name, laughing together, or giving our finances, LET IT ALL BE DONE to the glory of Jesus. We worship because we are reveling in His Grace and enjoying Him and wish to celebrate His matchless GLORY [Greek "Doxa" meaning His "manifested Presence."] whether gathered or scattered!

I'M THINKING - Wade Burleson got it right when he said this...

"Worship in many churches is either on life support or is dead. But it has nothing to do with whether saints play guitars versus Steinway pianos, or videos versus violins, or any other differences in style. Though many call the disagreements over 'contemporary' and 'traditional' styles of worship 'wars,' in reality, the REAL war in worship is the "internal battle in me." [All of us!] God calls me to rest in Him, to enjoy Him, TO BE SO captivated and enraptured by His love and grace for me, that I will burst unless I actively worship God and give expression to what's happening in my soul."

Wade goes on to say...

"Worship is an inner [spiritual] health made audible. If there is no soul-tingling, mind-bending, emotion-touching, will-transforming enjoyment of God, then there is no soul-tingling, mind-bending, emotion-touching, will-transforming worship of God! Worship of God is non-existent when enjoyment of God is non-existent. Sure, I can sing songs, play music, and 'do church,' but if there is no understanding of what it means to be fully satisfied in God, then there will be no desire on my part to publicly express my praise and gratitude in real worship of God." [Privately OR Corporately!]

Paul Burleson here...

I'M THINKING - I'll just quit typing and have a moment of worship myself.

IT'S SHOUTING TIME!"

Chapter 19: No Change of Your Scenery or Circumstances is Needed for Real Prosperity in the New Covenant

There is a promise from God in Jeremiah 29:11 that is often quoted and nearly always misinterpreted. God says, *"For I know the plans I have for you... plans to prosper you and not harm you...plans to give you hope and a future."*

Christians in the habit of plucking verses from their context are unable to tell you the circumstances surrounding this promise. For example, when was this promise given? To whom was God speaking? What occurred to cause God to make this promise? These three questions are examples of the things that should be asked before a Christian makes any assumptions. If you are claiming this promise in the belief and hope that God is about to change your environment for the better, then you have no understanding of its meaning.

It's important that you read the following two paragraphs very carefully. Too many Christians 'zone out' when it comes to history, but the diamonds in God's Word are only discovered after the necessary dirt work. "Bloom where you are planted" is an ancient phrase that has its roots in this Jer. 29:11 promise. I hope to show you that God may never change your environment, but your ability to "bloom" or personally prosper is never contingent on such change. That's the meaning of this Jeremiah 29:11 promise. Let me show you.

In 609 B.C. a very wicked and brutal empire took control of the world. The Babylonians (sometimes called Chaldeans in the Bible) defeated the ancient Assyrians and the Egyptians and took the stage as world conquerors. Two years later Babylonian King Nebuchadnezzar launched his first of three attacks against Jerusalem and the Jewish people (607 B.C. - 597 B.C. - 586 B.C.) Each successive attack during this 21-year time period was more brutal than the previous, ending in 586 B.C. with the destruction of the Jewish Temple and the desolation of the entire city of Jerusalem.

It was during Nebuchadnezzar's first aggressive move against Jerusalem (607 B.C.) that Daniel, his three friends (Shadrach, Meshach, and Abednego), and other Jewish leaders were taken captive. Ten years later (597 B.C.) Nebuchadnezzar came back to Jerusalem to get more Jews to assist the Babylonian Empire in building better roads, erecting stronger walls, and creating greater weapons.

Nebuchadnezzar didn't take all the Jews into captivity. Far more Jews remained in Jerusalem than were taken as prisoners, including the prophet Jeremiah who began placing a yoke around his neck proclaiming to God's people that the Babylonian captivity would last "until the seventy years for Babylon have expired" (Jeremiah 29:10 NAS).

Think about it. 70 years for Babylon to reign as a world empire. That's a long time for people to be held in Babylonian captivity. The United States war in Iraq has lasted a little over 10 years. Can you imagine having your husband, son or other loved one in Iraq without having the ability to see him or hear from him for decades? Or reverse the role. How would you like to be a young Jewish artisan or servant in the Babylonian Empire like Daniel and his friends, only to hear in a letter from Jeremiah that your captivity will only end after Babylon's 70-year world reign comes to an end?

More than a few Jews didn't like hearing Jeremiah's proclamations of a long captivity (Jeremiah 25:25). One such Jew was a priest and false prophet named Hananiah. He mocked Jeremiah's prophecy (see Jeremiah 28), ripped the wooden yoke off Jeremiah's neck, and told the people that "God told me the captivity would last just two more years" (Jeremiah 28:3). The Jews in Jerusalem began believing the false promise that God would change their circumstances soon.

It was at this time that God had Jeremiah send "a letter" to the captives in Babylon. The letter is what we know as Jeremiah 29. God knew that the false hope of quick release would make its way to His people in Babylon, so He speaks to them in Jeremiah 29:4-10:

"Thus says the Lord of hosts, the God of Israel, to all the exiles whom I have sent into exile from Jerusalem to Babylon, 'Build houses and live in them; and plant gardens and eat their produce (i.e. "bloom where you are planted"). *Take wives and become the fathers of sons and daughters, and take wives for your sons and give your daughters to husbands, that they may bear sons and daughters; and multiply there and do not decrease. Seek the welfare of the city where I have sent you into exile, and pray to the Lord on its behalf; for in its welfare you will have welfare.' For thus says the Lord of hosts, the God of Israel, 'Do not let your prophets who are in your midst and your diviners deceive you, and do not listen to the dreams which they dream. For they prophesy falsely to you in My name; I have not sent them,' declares the Lord. For thus says the Lord, 'When seventy years have been completed for Babylon, I will visit you and fulfill My good word to you, to bring you back to this place* (Jerusalem)."

Oh my. Only after these instructions to plant where you are, pray for your wicked masters, and be at peace with your environment does God give the Jeremiah 29:11 promise:

"For I know the plans that I have for you,' declares the Lord, 'plans for welfare and not for calamity to give you a future and a hope."

Oh boy. I'd like to ask you a question. Which prophecy inspires more hope? Is it Hananiah's false prophecy of captivity for less than two years? Or is it Jeremiah's prophecy to "bloom where you are planted" and experience a long captivity? Think before you answer. Babylon would last as an empire for 70 years. Jeremiah knew this, for God told him (see both Jeremiah 25:25 and Jeremiah 29:10). That means when Jeremiah sent his letter to the Jews in Babylon in 597 B.C. the Jews still had an additional fifty-eight years of captivity left. 58 years of captivity versus 2 years of captivity. Which prophecy sounds better to the Jews at first hearing?

The common trap laid for us by our enemy is the one where we measure our personal prosperity by how quickly God changes our environment for the better. It would be wise for us to stop assessing God's favor in this manner. God's purposes are much broader than our individual lives. That doesn't mean God doesn't care about me or you, for He does. He gave us His only Son. To "bloom where you are planted," is to trust that God knows the bigger picture and is at work on a grander scale, fulfilling a greater purpose that we can't even understand right now. So any measurement of my personal prosperity or God's favor for me must always be independent of my current circumstances. God is at work even when I can't see it.

One of the men who took Jeremiah's advice to "bloom where you are planted" was the prophet Daniel. We know, in fact, that Daniel often read Jeremiah's letters while he was in Babylonian captivity (see Daniel 9:2). Daniel listened and obeyed God's instructions. He built a house. He planted a garden for his produce. He prayed for the wicked kings of Babylon. He lived in peace. He was present at the king's palace in October 539 B.C. -- exactly 70 years after Babylon had become a world empire - when the hand of God wrote on the wall *"Mene, mene, tekel upharsin."*

That very night God's justice was executed against the Babylonians and the Babylonian Empire came to an end. God had led His servant Cyrus, King of Persia, to divert the Euphrates River and the Persian army crawled under the great walls of Babylon on a dry river bed and took the city as their own. God's purpose for Babylon was over.

Daniel never left Persia to go back to Jerusalem, even though Cyrus allowed the Jews to return and rebuild the Temple and their city. Daniel's tomb is in Susa (Iran), the ancient capital of Persia (modern Iran). Because the Persians loved Daniel's ability to "foresee the future," they deemed him the greatest "magi" of all. The Persians revered Daniel, kept his scrolls in Persia and studied them at their universities.

The magi in the east came to understand through reading Daniel's scroll (the book of Daniel), that a great King - a King above all Kings - would be born among the Jews. Five hundred years after Daniel's death, magi from the ancient Babylonian and Persian Empire lands (e.g. "magi from the east") came to Jerusalem and asked Herod:

"Where is He who is born King of the Jews" (Matthew 2:2)

The magi eventually sought Jesus because Daniel bloomed where he was planted.

I propose that if you find yourself in a difficult situation that God seems in no hurry to change, and you learn like the ancient Jews to "bloom where you are planted," there will come a day when those around you will come looking for your King.

That's your greater purpose.

Chapter 20: Piercing and Removing the Veil of Your Shame in the New Covenant

The Law is summed up in this saying: "Love your neighbor as yourself." Romans 13:9

Recently I was at a marriage conference when the speaker said something that made both my and my wife's backs tighten and our shoulder muscles spasm. He said, "Ladies and gentleman, the reason you don't love your spouse is because you don't love God with all your heart. If you loved God more, you'd love your spouse more."

Ugh.

Anytime I hear someone say, "Just love God more -- with all your heart, soul, and mind -- and all your problems will be solved," I want to stand up and shout, "You don't get it! The Law is never summarized or fulfilled by loving God more. The Law is summarized and fulfilled by loving your neighbor as yourself."

If you are struggling right now in any human relationship - be it marriage, parental, sibling, neighbor, church member, or work - you might want to think carefully about why Paul never summarizes the Law with an encouragement to "love God more."

What is the Law?

When the Bible speaks of "the Law" it references all that is contained in the Five Books of the Law - Genesis, Exodus, Leviticus, Numbers, and Deuteronomy. In the Bible "the Law" is sometimes called "Moses" because the first five books are attributed to Moses.

When Jesus walked with the two men on the road to Emmaus, they did not recognize Him. Listen to what Jesus did:

"And beginning with Moses (the Law) and the Prophets, He explained to them what was said in all the Scriptures concerning Himself" (Luke 24:27).

It drives me bananas when Christians try to artificially separate the Law of Moses into a moral portion (the 10 Commandments), a ceremonial portion (the Feasts and the sacrifices) and a civil portion (the yearly calendar, the new moon festivals) portions, urging Christians to keep "certain parts of the Law" – for example "the Sabbath" – to show their "love for God."

The Law is not about anyone's love for God. The Law is about God's love for us in Jesus Christ. The Law - all of it - concerns Jesus Christ. In Genesis Jesus is the lamb slain for Adam and Eve to cover their sins as well as the ram at Abraham's altar. In Exodus, He's the Passover lamb and the Ark that leads God's children to the Promised Land. In Leviticus, Jesus is the High Priest and the Sacrifices that make at-one-ment for the people of God. In Numbers, He's the Cloud by Day and Pillar of Fire by night and the Living Water that comes from the Rock. In Deuteronomy, Jesus is the City of our REFUGE and the Law itself. I could go on, and on, and on.... The Law is all about Christ.

Since the Law is about Jesus Christ and God's love for us, when the Apostle Paul "summarizes" the Law - or declares the Law is fulfilled - it is always a reference to the love of God for us in Christ. This is really good news for people who struggle with shame.

The Blackness Within

A person filled with shame constantly feels and hears the message "I can't..." or "I'll never..." or "I'm incapable..." or "It's hopeless." A shame-filled person is one who feels helpless to change. The best way I've ever heard it described is "a blackness within." Once a person filled with shame begins to spiral downward in relationships, there's no way out - it's all black. It's either "fight" or "flight." A shame-filled person must either control or run.

To tell a person who is filled with shame and who is struggling in his or her human relationships to simply "love God more" only drives that person deeper into darkness. They can't. "To love God more' is an encouragement that only deepens the hearers' descent into darkness. Even worse, to tell others they should "love God more" in order to repair their broken human relationships is an absolute misunderstanding of how the Bible summarizes the Law and calls our attention to how the Law is fulfilled.

Listen to the Apostle Paul again: "The Law is summed up in this saying: "Love your neighbor as yourself" (Romans 13:9). Paul does not "sum up" (Gk. ἀνακεφαλαιοῦται) the Law by saying, "Love God with all your heart and your neighbor as yourself." Nope. He skips "loving God" completely and says the Law is "summed up" in "love your neighbor as yourself." He makes his argument even stronger in Galatians 5:14 when he says "the entire Law is fulfilled in one statement: Love your neighbor as yourself." The word "fulfilled" (Gk. πεπλήρωται) is much stronger than "sum up." The verb "fulfilled" is in the past perfect tense which literally makes the verse say "When you love your neighbor as yourself "the Law" has already been fulfilled.

This side of the cross, the Law is only summarized and fulfilled when you "love your neighbor as yourself." The question for every believer in Jesus Christ: "How can I deeply love others as well as myself?"

Lifting the Veil of Shame

If the Law is all about Jesus Christ and God's love for us (and it is), then the only way we'll ever find healing in our human relationships is not to love God more, but to learn to rest in God's love for us through Jesus Christ (the Law).

Someone has said there are five languages of love. Stop thinking about how much you love God, and start thinking about how much He loves you. Think about God's love for you in Christ according to the five languages. STOP! Change the tape playing in your mind right now. Don't even dare think about how much you love God in these next few moments and contemplate in the following verses how much God loves you!

(1). Words of affection

God says to you "I have loved you with an everlasting love" (Jeremiah 31:3). He declares "You are the apple of my eye" (Zechariah 2:8). God encourages us with "Fear not, for I am with you; be not dismayed, for I am your God; I will strengthen you, I will help you, I will uphold you with my righteous (Isaiah 41:10). John reminds us that true love is seen in God's love for us, not our love for God, for "this is love, not that we love God, but that He loved us and sent us His Son" (I John 4:8).

(2). Quality time

"The LORD himself goes before you and will be with you, for He says, 'I will never leave you nor forsake you. Do not be afraid; do not be discouraged.'" (Deut. 31:8) "Keep your lives free from the love of money and be content with what you have, because God has said, "Never will I leave you; never will I forsake you." (Hebrews 13:5). This verse from Hebrews contains five negatives - "I will never, no never, no never leave you nor forsake you." That's quality time.

(3). Acts of service

"God who made the world and all things in it, since He is Lord of heaven and earth, does not dwell in temples made with hands; nor is He served by human hands, as though He needed anything, since He Himself gives to all people life and breath and all things" (Acts

17:24-25). There's nothing God needs from you. There's no act of service or devotion you can give that can make God pleased, for He is pleased with Himself. He's the One who "gives to you life, breath, and all things." He's the One who works all things "for your good" (Romans 8:28).

(4). Physical touch

"But you are not in the flesh, you are in the Spirit, since the Spirit of God really dwells in you" (Romans 8:9). It is "the life of God in the soul of man" that is your hope. He who is "in you is greater than he who is in the world" (I John 4:4). He numbers the very hairs on your head, and knows you intimately. As for us, "we now only see Him as a reflection in a mirror; but there's coming a Day when we shall see Him face to face. Now I know in part; then I shall know fully, even as I am fully known now" (I Corinthians 13:12).

(5). Special gifts

"He who did not spare his own Son, but gave him up for us all--how will he not also, along with him, graciously give us all things?" (Romans 8:32). "God will supply all my needs according to His riches in Christ" (Phil. 4:19). It's amazing that all the promises of God are "a resounding Yes!" in Christ (II Corinthians 1:20), so I never have to work for the blessings, favor and pleasure of God, but simply must learn to rest in the fulfillment of the Law (Jesus Christ).

Chapter 21: Shame and the Imago Dei (The Image of God) in the New Covenant

There's a current of fear raging in my soul.
It prevents me believing I'll ever be whole.
It's an inner sorrow that some call "shame,"
And is seen in my game of affixing blame.

I fight to be seen as the one without error,
For allegations of fault bring me to terror;
Fear you will discover what I already sense,
"I am defective" and perfection is defense.

When I point my finger and judge you for sin,
It is really a cover for my fear flowing within.
Shame screams in my mind "I am defective,"
And from this pain comes my ugly invective.

If I've lost control and I'm full of anger.
The one you love may now be a stranger.
I'm struggling to grasp God's truth for me,
How knowing His Word can set me free.

He says I'm made in His image and bear His grace,
I'm the apple of His eye and He's taken my place.
He'd never love and die for one without worth, So
please pray I come to know my value from birth.

The demon of shame drives my inner fear,
Arguing there's no way God holds me dear,
But when I can believe God over my shame,
I can love you as is and end my deadly game.

W.W. Burleson 2016

Author's Note: The preceding poem, *Shame and the Imago Dei*, was written by the author in 2016 in response to the request for help from a loved one who struggled with understanding why sudden emotional outbursts occurred. I was told the poem helped immensely.

Chapter 22: When I Begin to Understand the New Covenant, a Loved Me Begins Leaking Love

When you begin to understand how much God loves you, you begin to love yourself. Think about it. Those who are loved are the ones who come to love themselves. I'm not talking about selfishness; I'm talking about self-love.

There's a difference. Jesus calls you to love yourself, because you can't love others well until you love yourself (e.g. "love your neighbor as yourself"). When you begin resting in God's love - instead of constantly measuring your love for God - you begin to understand just how much you really count in this universe.

God didn't die for worms. He died for His bride.

He died for those He chose from eternity to redeem, those He's making co-heirs with Christ. God has loved you with an everlasting love, and it is this love of God for you in Christ that is the fulfillment of the Law. It is the essence of the Law, for the Law is all about Jesus Christ.

So, when you begin to understand the Law (Christ), you begin to rest in God's love. And when you become so saturated with the love of God for you - and not so doggone consumed with your puny attempts to love God - you can't help but love others. Jesus said, "It is by your love for one another that all will know you know Me" (John 13:35). Unfortunately, many Christians don't love one another because we get in a measuring contest about how much we love God rather than teaching people to rest in God's love for us in Jesus Christ.

For those who wish to argue, "But wait a minute! Jesus said, 'Love the Lord your God with all your heart and with all your soul and with all your mind" (Matthew 22:37). How can you say, Wade, that it's not about our love for God?" Answer: Nobody loves God with every ounce of heart, soul and mind - except Christ. Nobody will ever love God like that - except Christ. This is why Christ is the fulfillment of the Law; this is why Christ alone earns all the blessings from God due full obedience to the Law.

In the new agreement with God under which we all now abide (the New Covenant), God's blessings are given to us via our union with Christ, and the only way we'll ever come to the place of even beginning to learn what it means to live life fully is to focus on the fulfillment of the Law (Jesus Christ) and God's incredible, eternal, unconditional, and supremely personal love for us through Christ! When the Bible speaks of the fulfillment of the Law in the New Testament, it is all about our love for others - and our love for God is not ever mentioned - because the Law is about us coming to an understanding of God's love for us in Jesus Christ - the Christ of God who is the fulfillment of the Law!

Summary

If you are filled with shame and experiencing broken relationships, I hope that this little chapter helps pierce the veil of darkness. The Law (God's love for you in Christ) has been fulfilled when you love others as much as you love yourself, but you can't begin to love your shame-filled self until you know how much God loves you! However, once saturated and wet with an understanding and enjoyment of God's love for you, you can't help but get others wet with love when they rub up next to you because you are leaking the only real Love that lasts - God's love for you!

Next time you feel tempted to focus on yours or another's love for God, why don't you give it a rest and give this shame-filled world some really good news. Why don't you help pierce the veil of shame and move people out of the darkness and help them discover the incredible riches of God's love for us in Christ!

Chapter 23: We're Promised Peace in Chaos in the New Covenant, Not Peace from Chaos

In 1969 Paul Simon wrote a song entitled *Bridge Over Troubled Waters*. The closing words of that are "Like a bridge over troubled waters, I will ease your mind." Pop culture often weeds its way into the garden of truth. In my thirty years of pastoral ministry, I've seen more than a few Christians create a Jesus who becomes their "bridge over troubled waters." A typical prayer meeting is proof. Most requests are for Jesus to remove troubles such as illness, poverty, conflict, etc. It's as if Christians believe the world around them is peaceful by nature, and intrusions of trouble and turmoil are unnatural.

Not so.

That the world evolves peacefully, gradually, and uniformly toward better and better outcomes is a lie of those who whose sole hope is mankind. It is an unscientific belief-- unscientific because it is neither observable, measurable nor verifiable -- and it has led people to believe that this world is naturally evolving toward better outcomes. Mankind, it is said, is a microcosm of Mother Universe and her progression toward stability and peace.

Not so.

Mankind, apart from God, is always devolving -- like the universe -- toward worse and worse outcomes.

The brilliant Immanuel Velikovsky, a close friend of Albert Einstein, shook the scientific world with his 1950's book *Worlds in Collision*, where Velikovsky proved the earth's human population has almost been destroyed three times throughout history by natural, cosmic disasters. Velikovsky, a Jew, was deemed a heretic for his postulations that the sun used to rise in the west and set in the east, that the ancients wrote in great detail how destructive forces from the skies totally destroyed the world as it was then known, and that the Old Testament accounts of "the sun standing still" and "great stones from heaven" crushing the earth are nothing more than the destructive gravity forces of near collisions with stellar objects, including the newest planet Venus.

The world, wrote Velikovsky, is a world in chaos.

Jesus agrees.

Jesus told us that we will "always have the poor with us" (Matt. 26:11).The Apostle Paul, assuming everyone knew the world is in chaos, wrote "the whole creation is groaning, waiting for the day of redemption" (Romans 8:22). He further wrote, "Don't be shaken by the troubles you are going through. You know that we are destined for such troubles" (I Thess. 3:3). The writer of Hebrews commends those with faith in God who were "tortured, refusing to be released so that they might gain an even better resurrection. Others faced jeers and flogging, and even chains and imprisonment. They were put to death by stoning; they were sawed in two; they were killed by the sword. They went about in sheepskins and goatskins, destitute, persecuted and mistreated— the world was not worthy of them. They wandered in deserts and mountains, living in caves and in holes in the ground" (Hebrews 11:35-38). Jesus wasn't a bridge over troubled waters for these people. He brought them peace in the midst of their troubles.

Application

There is a growing sense among scientists that great natural disasters are coming. The evil of ISIS is spreading. The world economies - built on the lies of human governments and fiat currencies - is ready to collapse in an inescapable downward spiral.

It's coming.

But here's the thing worth remembering. Throughout the history of the world, these events have always come. The world is in chaos. This isn't anything new, nor does it necessarily indicate the end of the world and the second coming of Jesus Christ. Nobody knows if God's plans for this earth are coming to a close or will continue indefinitely.

What we do know is Jesus promised His followers a "peace that passes all understanding." Unless your theology of Jesus and His Kingdom transcends your temporal desire for life, health and happiness, you will always be shaken by chaos in this life. But if you know the God whose "Kingdom never ends" and believe that this life is only a step into the next, then you will not clutch to the absence of chaos as evidence of Christ's love for you.

Jesus is not our bridge over troubled waters; He's the stability of our souls and the Rock of our hope right smack dab in the middle of the turmoil around us.

Chapter 24: The Best Thing You Can Ask Jesus for in the New Covenant

There are only two times in the New Testament when Jesus says to someone, "What do you want me to do for you?"

Imagine.

Imagine if the Creator of the universe asks you personally, "What do you want me to do for you?" It reminds me of the old joke of the man walking on the beach and he finds a bottle with a genie inside, and ... well, you know where I'm going. What if God posed this question to you? How do you think you would respond?

It fascinated me to discover that the two occasions where Jesus asks this question are both found in Mark 10. The first time he asks two of His disciples, James and John, "What do you want me to do for you" (Mark 10:36) and they responded:

"Grant that we may sit, one on Your right and one on Your left, in Your glory" (Mark 10:37).

What was it they were wanting? From Jesus response, we gather that James and John wanted the power and authority of Jesus. They wished to "sit with authority" over others in the Kingdom. The way Jesus responded to their request reveals what Jesus thinks about so-called "spiritual authority." He says to James and John, "you don't know what you are asking," and then responds with these sharp words:

"You know that those who are recognized as rulers of the Gentiles lord over them; and their great men exercise authority over them. But it is not this way among you. Whoever wishes to become great among you shall be your servant; and whoever wishes to be first among you shall be the slave of all. For even the Son of Man did not come to be served, but to serve, and to give His life a ransom for many." (Mark 10:41-45).

Jesus rebuked James and John for wanting to "exercise authority over others." I've said before, and I'll say it again, the greatest problem in evangelical Christianity today is the desire for pastors, elders, and "spiritual leaders" to exercise spiritual authority or power over God's people. This is not the way it's supposed to be, at least according to Jesus.

The second time Jesus asks the question "What do you want me to do for you" is just a few verses later in Mark 10. There is a blind man waiting on the side of the road as Jesus walks out of Jericho heading to Jerusalem. His name is Bartimaeus. The blind man responds to Jesus by saying:

"I want to see..."

Jesus then commends Bartimaeus for His faith and heals the blind man. So, in the same chapter we have Jesus asking two times "What do you want me to do for you?" The first time he asks, his disciples, James and John, answer "We want to sit with authority" and Jesus rebukes them. The second times He asks, the blind man Bartimaeus responds, "I want to see with clarity" and Jesus praises him.

Preachers, we must learn well the lesson of Mark 10.

Desiring bigger influence over people, or wanting more "spiritual authority," or asking God to give you a church or a group of believers who will recognize your authority and do what you say ("because the preacher is our spiritual authority") is a desire that seems ripe for Divine rebuke.

However, praying that you might "see with clarity" the wisdom of God is a prayer Jesus honors. When we acknowledge our weakness and turn to Jesus for clarity, we are only concerned with our ability to see, never others willingness to follow.

I'd rather be like blind Bartimaeus than James and John. I want to see with clarity and not even think of having any so-called spiritual authority.

Chapter 25: Why Women ARE NOT to Keep Silent in the New Covenant

A cult is defined as a group of people who follow a particular system of religious behavior established by an authoritative or revered person. Lest someone argue that Christianity is a cult, remember that Jesus said, "You shall know the truth and the truth shall set you free."

Jesus frees people, cult leaders bind people. Jesus speaks truth to people, cult leaders lie to people. Jesus empowers people, cult leaders oppress people. Christianity is not a cult nor is Jesus a cult leader. He saves His people from systems that bind.

Some Christian men, however, have set themselves up as authorities in the institutional church and implemented systems of control that turn pockets of evangelicalism into cultism. The most prominent example of cultism within evangelical Christianity is the system of behavior imposed on women within the ecclesia (assembly) of Christ.

Christian women are told by some authoritative church leaders that "women must never teach men; women must be silent in the assembly; women must not have any authority over men, and women should seek to be passive servants to, and receivers of, male leadership, but should never exhibit characteristics of vibrant leadership when males are present."

This system of behavior for women is cultic; for it is definitely not Christian nor is it consistent with the teachings of Scripture.

The Scriptures and the Freedom of Women

The New Testament gives many examples of women teaching men (cf. Luke 2:25-38; Acts 21:9; John 4:28-29). Women served as deaconia in the early church (cf. Romans 16:1-2). Women were co-laborers with men in Christ's kingdom (cf. Romans 16:3) and at least one of Christ's apostles was a woman (cf. Romans 16:7). Males and females accompanied Jesus throughout His earthly ministry (cf. Luke 8:1-3).

Gifted men and women spread the good news of the kingdom. God first used women to preach (proclaim) the resurrection of His Son (cf. John 20:1-2). Male disciples later proclaimed the resurrected Christ in the same manner female disciples first preached Him (cf. Luke 24:1-11). Women in the upper room at Pentecost received the same Spirit and the same gifts as men (cf. Acts 1:14-15). God is emphatic that in the days of the New Covenant both males and females will prophesy of Him (cf. Acts 2:17-18). The Apostle Paul encouraged men and women to teach, to pray and to fully participate in the assembly (cf. I Corinthians 11:4-5 and I Corinthians 14:23-24).

God clearly reveals to us that Christian men and women should serve as they are gifted by the Spirit. Any imposed restrictions on women speaking, teaching, or leading in the assembly of Christ is contrary to inspired revelation of God's word. So if the New Testament teaches that men and women are gifted by the Spirit to do the work of the kingdom, why do some put a system of restrictions on women, a system totally contrary to the overall tenor and explicit teachings of holy Scripture?

Stupid, Stupid, Stupid

Several years ago I was called by the Tulsa Police Department to a home where a young man committed suicide by cutting off his right hand with a pocket knife and bleeding out. We found him dead with his head slumped to his chest and a pool of blood at his feet. Before the young man died he laid his pocket knife in the middle of an open Bible with these words underlined: "And if your right hand causes you to sin, cut if off and throw it away. It is better for you to lose one part of your body than for your whole body to be thrown in hell" (Matthew 5:30).

I will never forget the gruesomeness of discovering the young man's right hand in a trash can, nor the words of the lieutenant as he walked around the room muttering under his breath, "Stupid, stupid, stupid." We were later told that the man had struggled for years with pornography and masturbation. The man took the words of the Bible and obeyed them. However, there is something mighty stupid about a man who reads Scripture and acts on words without taking time to look at their meaning, particularly when the overall tenor and teaching of Scripture is opposite of the action he is compelled to take!

If anybody ever tells you that women should never teach men, or that women should never be in leadership over men, or that women should be silent around men, then you should be kind to that person (as always), but possibly mutter under your breath about such ideas, "Stupid, stupid, stupid." These people, well-intentioned as they may be, are committing spiritual suicide by acting on words of Scripture without looking at their meaning. The system they seek to impose is opposite to the overall tenor and teachings of Scripture on the subject of women (see above). Below are some the verses some misuse and create environments conducive to spiritual death:

"In like manner also, see that women adorn themselves in modest apparel, with shamefacedness and sobriety; not with braided hair, or gold, or pearls, or costly array; but (which becometh women professing godliness) with good works. Let the woman learn in silence with all subjection. But I suffer not a woman to teach, nor to usurp authority over the man, but to be in silence. For Adam was first formed, then Eve. And Adam was not deceived, but the woman being deceived was in the transgression. Notwithstanding she shall be saved in childbearing, if they continue in faith and charity and holiness with sobriety" (I Timothy 2:9-15).

I recently had a Christian man paraphrase for me I Timothy 2:9-15 and then tell me, "I will never have a woman lead me, teach me, or allow myself to be in a position where women usurp my authority over them because I believe the Bible!" My friend has the problem of reading words of Scripture and acting on them without taking the time to understand their meaning.

Until you understand the problem Timothy faced (the man to whom the words in I Timothy 2:9-15 are written), and until you are familiar with Ephesus (the place where Timothy lived), and until you have a working knowledge of the Amazons (the warrior women that the ancient Greeks believed founded Ephesus), and until you comprehend the influence of the cult of Artemis and the Temple of Artemis which was in Ephesus, the meaning of the Apostle Paul's words will never be rightly understood.

F. F. Bruce once said, "Subjugation of a woman is a system of man's fallen nature. If the work of Christ involves... breaking the fall, then the implication of His work for the liberation of women is plain."

Jesus Christ came to liberate subjugated women. The cultism in evangelicalism regarding women's behaviors will only be broken when people lay aside stupid, false obedience to I Timothy 2:9-14 and realize the meaning of Paul's words to Timothy.

Ephesus and the Temple of Artemis

Rachelle and I went with a group of friends to visit the ruins of ancient Ephesus (located in southwest Turkey) recently. Ephesus was the location of the most magnificent of the Seven Wonders of the Ancient World--The Temple of Artemis.

This is the first temple in the world made completely of marble. The richest man in the world in his day, King Croesus (595-547 B.C.) of Lydia (modern Turkey), ordered the Temple of Artemis be constructed in honor of the Greek goddess Artemis. Work on the Temple of Artemis began in 550 B.C. and took over a century to complete. King Croesus lived long enough to stuff the foundation of the Temple of Artemis with tens of thousands of gold coins to serve as talismans, ensuring the Temple's protection from destruction. Generations of people, even in America, have used the phrase "Rich as Croesus" to describe wealthy people in their day. King Croesus is given credit by many historians as the inventor of gold and silver coinage. His wealth is legendary, and he gave his riches to fund the building of the Temple of Artemis.

Croesus was a contemporary of Cyrus the Great, the founder of the Persian Empire. Cyrus was the king who defeated the Babylonians, freeing the Jews from their Babylonian captivity, enabling them to return to Jerusalem to rebuild Solomon's Temple. Therefore, the Temple of Artemis and the Second Temple in Jerusalem were built during the same time period (the 6th century B.C.).

However, it was only the Temple of Artemis that became one of the Seven Wonders of the Ancient World because of its stunning beauty. The Temple of Artemis was a temple dedicated to the power, beauty and strength of women. Marble artisans from all over the world carved Amazon women into the base of the 120 columns. Amazons were "warrior women" from an area north of Ephesus and the Black Sea (modern Ukraine). These Amazon women were known for their fierce fighting ability and had been made famous by the Greek poet Homer in his portrayal of them in The Iliad.

Homer (c. 750 B.C.) also gave tribute in The Iliad to Artemis, the Greek goddess of women and of war. Artemis is called by Homer "Artemis the Hunter, Queen of the Wild Beasts" (Iliad 21.470). Artemis is also presented as the goddess Phosphorous or Light (Strabo, Geo. 1.9.). If worshiped properly and prayed to during childbirth, Artemis promised to deliver women from death while giving birth. For this reason, women in the ancient world revered and worshiped Artemis.

Likewise, men worshiped Artemis during times of battle and war. Since the ancient world was always at war, Artemis was often on the lips of men during times of battle. The Greek men (and later the Romans) prayed to Artemis (the Romans called her Diana), not

Apollo in times of battle. In Greek mythology, Zeus fathered the twins Artemis and Apollo through the Titaness Leto. The Artemis cult taught that Artemis was superior to Apollo because she came (was born) born first.

When men and women entered the Temple of Artemis in Ephesus, the women would wear fancy hair braids, bedeck themselves with jewelry and ornate clothes as they prayed to Artemis. Heliodorus said, "Their locks of hairs carry their prayers." There were no sacrifices in this Temple. The women worshiped Artemis with their clothing, jewelry, and their words. Artemis, in turn, gave them their sexual prowess over men and their deliverance during childbirth. Likewise, men came to Artemis, acknowledging their need of her strength during time of war.

The men would hold up hands, palms up, just above their waist as they prayed for victory in battle. Not surprisingly Ephesus, above all other places in the ancient world, celebrated the power, strength and beauty of women and their ability to use their sexual prowess to manipulate and dominate men. The Temple operations, which included prostitution and craftsmen who sold gold and silver idols of Artemis, drove the economy of Ephesus. Hundreds of thousands of people visited the city annually.'

Paul and Timothy's Presence in Ephesus in the Midst of the Artemis Cult

Acts 18:24 through Acts 20:1 records for us that Paul and Timothy spent three years in Ephesus (c. A.D. 55-58), by far the longest time Paul spent in any one city during his three missionary journeys. Paul almost lost his life during a riot in the city because silversmiths who made little statues of the goddess Artemis were upset that Paul and Timothy were cutting into their business by winning converts to Christianity. Paul would later write in I Corinthians 15:32 that he "fought wild beasts at Ephesus." Did he fight lions, tigers and bears? No, the wild beasts were the people of Ephesus who were devoted to Artemis, "The Queen of the Wild Beasts."

When Paul left Ephesus in A.D. 58, he traveled south for about 30 miles to the island of Miletus and then called for wise leaders of the church in Ephesus to join him at Miletus where he said to them, "After I leave, savage wolves will come among you and will not spare the flock. Even some among you will arise and distort the truth to draw away disciples after them" (cf. Acts 20:29-30).

Sure enough, less than five years later (A.D. 63) the Christians in Ephesus were in trouble. There were some women or maybe even a single woman, most likely a new convert out of the Artemis cult, who had begun to teach false truth in the assembly at Ephesus. Timothy is sent to Ephesus to help the church and give some correction. Timothy sends to Paul a letter from Ephesus, giving Paul an update on what is happening and asking some specific questions about how he should proceed (a letter that is not extant). The Apostle Paul sends a response to Timothy, a letter we now call I Timothy.

It's important to remember (as we have seen) that nowhere in Scripture does Jesus, Paul or any other apostle restrict women in the assembly. In fact, when a false teacher nicknamed Jezebel begins to have influence among believers in the city of Thyatira, Jesus does not reprimand the church for having a female teacher, but rather He upbraids the church for not doing anything about her false teaching (cf. Revelation 2:24).

The Meaning of I Timothy 2:9-15

Now, let's put up I Timothy 2:9-15 again in order to discover the meaning of the words in light of what we know about the Artemis cult in Ephesus:

"In like manner also, see that women adorn themselves in modest apparel, with shamefacedness and sobriety; not with braided hair, or gold, or pearls, or costly array; but (which becometh women professing godliness) with good works. Let the woman learn in silence with all subjection. But I suffer not a woman to teach, nor to usurp authority over the man, but to be in silence. For Adam was first formed, then Eve. And Adam was not deceived, but the woman being deceived was in the transgression. Notwithstanding she shall be saved in childbearing, if they continue in faith and charity and holiness with sobriety."(I Timothy 2:9-15)

1). *"Let the women adorn themselves in modest apparel"* (v. 9).

Obviously, there were women coming to the assembly of Christ in Ephesus similar to the way they used to go to the Temple of Artemis, dressed to kill, with braided hair, gold, pearls and fine clothing. Paul is letting Timothy know that this mode of dress, particularly in the city of Ephesus, was not conducive to the worship of Christ. What Christ desires is the beauty of goodness toward others, not the drawing attention to oneself in public.

2). *"Let the woman learn in silence with all subjection"* (v. 11).

The reason I believe the problem in Ephesus is a particular woman who is in a teaching position within the assembly of Christ is because the noun "woman" is in the singular, not the plural. In verses 9 and 10, women is in the plural, but in verse 11, Paul switches to "the woman" or possibly that woman about whom Timothy has written Paul. It can't be a universal prohibition for all time against all women ever teaching men in the assembly because (a). That would violate the tenor and teaching of the rest of Scripture where women frequently taught men, and (b). Paul has elsewhere encouraged men and women to teach, to pray and to fully participate in the assembly as they are gifted (cf. I Corinthians 11:4-5 and I Corinthians 14:23-24).

Further, the word translated silence is *hesuchia* (quietness). It is used in I Timothy 2:2 to describe what the character of every believer should be, both males and females. It never means "don't speak," but addresses the character of humility. This woman in Ephesus, coming out of a society saturated with the power, strength, abilities and even domination of women through the

Artemis cult, needed to realize that she had a great deal to learn about Christ and His kingdom.

3). *"I suffer not a woman to teach, nor to usurp authority over the man, but to be in silence"* (v. 12).

This is the key phrase. First, the phrase translated "I suffer not a woman to teach" is literally in the tense of "I am not now permitting a woman to teach." Again, the woman not now permitted to teach is in the singular. It is the same woman of verse 11. This woman needs to learn in quiet humility before she ever presumes to teach, because she is still too influenced by Artemis cultic beliefs. This verse can NEVER be used as a proof text for women never teaching men or having "authority" over men.

a. Deborah gave counsel and taught men and women about the Law of God (cf. Judges 2:16-19; 4:1-5:31). Huldah prophesied to Israel the word of the Lord and led the men of Israel (2 Kings 22:14-20). Priscilla and Aquila explained more perfectly to Apollos the way of God in Ephesus (cf. Acts 18:19-26). Most importantly, when Jezebel was teaching error to the church in Thyatira, Jesus never once told the church they were wrong for having a woman teach or lead them; He simply said they were wrong for not rejecting her false teaching (Revelation 2:18-29).

b. "I suffer not a woman .... to usurp authority over the man" (v. 13).

This phrase "usurp authority" translates one Greek word *authentein*. This word is used only one time in all of Scripture--let me repeat that again--this word authentein is used only once in the entire Bible, right here in I Timothy 2:12. This word was used, however, in classical Greek literature and it meant "to murder someone." Paul could have chosen nearly fifty Greek words to speak of the ordinary exercise of authority, but he chose a word that more represents someone "dominating, controlling, or subjecting one to harm."

Of course, this is precisely what the Artemis cult taught women to do. Artemis was the female goddess of fertility and war. Women in Ephesus were taught to use their voices, their charm, their sexuality and their beauty to dominate, control and subjugate men. It seems that this woman in Ephesus was causing trouble in the church by behavior in the assembly of Christ that was way too similar to the ways of the Artemis cult from whence she came.

4). *"For Adam was formed first, then Eve"* (v. 13).

Timothy, tell the woman causing problems that her notion she should always have the floor and direct the assembly because she believes women are superior to men--since Artemis came first and Apollo came second--is a misguided belief. The truth is God created man first then He formed Eve from Adam, so it is very appropriate for her, a woman who considers herself a descendent of the Amazons, to sit quietly and learn from those who are older and wiser, even if they are males! Artemis taught the power of women to dominate men through sexual prowess, but Christ teaches that men are equal to women and there's nothing wrong with a woman learning from others (even men) before she begins to teach men.

5). *"And Adam was not deceived, but the woman being deceived was in the transgression"* (v. 14).

And Timothy, remind her that the Scriptures teach that Eve was deceived. Contrary to what she learned in the Temple of Artemis, males are not always her problem. To be deceived and in need of correction is just as much a possibility for her as it was for Eve. She must move away from her belief in female superiority, a belief reinforced by the Artemis cult.

6). *"Notwithstanding she shall be saved in childbearing, if they continue in faith and charity and holiness with sobriety"* (v. 15).

Timothy, tell this woman that she will be okay during childbirth, even if she totally and fully renounces her trust in Artemis. Yes, she lives in a culture that teaches Artemis alone saves a woman from death during childbirth, but the truth is Christ holds the keys of life

and death. When women continue in faith, hope and love--
avoiding the sexual immodesty and looseness on display in the
Temple of Artemis and the worship of the goddess of fertility and
war--it will be the one true God who delivers them from death
during childbirth, not Artemis.

7). And finally, Timothy, I wrote this letter to help you with the
problems in the assembly in honor of *"Him who alone has
immortality and dwells in unapproachable light, whom no man has
ever seen or can see"* (I Timothy 6:16).

The people of Ephesus called Artemis the goddess of Light. The
men approached Artemis in the Temple with hands raised above
their waist praying for victory in battle and in war. Paul reminded
Timothy in this same chapter that Christian men should approach
Christ in worship with their hands raised and pray for peace with
all men, not war. (Timothy 2:5). Christian women, come before
Christ with a sense of modesty and humility, realizing that the ways
of Christ are opposite of the ways of Artemis.

Paul's entire personal letter to Timothy was an encouragement to
him to "fight the wild beasts of Ephesus" and be faithful to the
gospel of Jesus Christ and correct the errors brought into the
church by "savage wolves" who were remaining under the
influence of Artemis theology.

Chapter 26: God Doesn't Always Do What I Ask in the New Covenant, but He's Already Done Far More than I'll Grasp

There are few things more gut-wrenching than losing a child to death because of illness or accident. A comparable pain might be the sudden death or unexpected critical illness of a spouse. Losing a parent to death--regardless of age--also brings to us a great deal of emotional trauma.

Precisely because the loss of a loved one is so painful, many turn to God when they begin to "walk through the valley of the shadow of death." Even people unaccustomed to prayer often ask God to heal their loved ones. In some cases, prayer chains are started, all doubts are cast out, and by faith Christian people claim and believe that God is going to heal those they love.

And yet death still comes.

Often the greater pain becomes my disappointment with God. The hardest question is always "Why?" Why does God not do what I ask? Why does God not answer my heartfelt pleas?

There seems to be some encouragement for those of us who ask the "Why" questions from a story in Luke 7:11-15 that involves a widow, her dead son, and Jesus.

Soon afterward He went to a city called Nain; and His disciples were going along with Him, accompanied by a large crowd. Now as He approached the gate of the city, a dead man was being carried out, the only son of his mother, and she was a widow; and a sizeable crowd from the city was with her. When the Lord saw her, He felt compassion for her, and said to her, "Do not weep." And He came up and touched the coffin; and the bearers came to a halt. And He said, "Young man, I say to you, arise!" The dead man sat up and began to speak. And Jesus gave him back to his mother.

You might be thinking, "But I thought this text was supposed to encourage me when God doesn't do what I ask? It looks to me like God did precisely what the widow desired--He healed her son. How is that help to us for whom God doesn't respond with a miracle?"

Let me see if I can't show you something pretty incredible (in my opinion) about the widow from Nain and the resurrection of her only son.

The Parallelism with Christ's Death

Jesus Christ raised three people from the dead during His earthly ministry--this son of the widow of Nain; the daughter of Jairus; and Lazarus. This resurrection of the widow's son was the first resurrection miracle Jesus performed. On many fronts, this miracle of the resurrected widow's son pictures and parallels God's compassion for us through the death and resurrection of Jesus Christ.

1. He was an only son. The Greek phrase used to describe this widow's son -- ὁ μονογενὴς υἱός literally "only begotten son"- is the same phrase used regarding Jesus in John 3:16. It is used only one other time in the New Testament, describing Abraham's son Isaac in Hebrews 11:17 when Abraham offered his "only begotten son" on the altar - a clear type of God the Father offering His Son as a sacrifice for us.

2. He was outside the gate. Both the widow's son and Jesus Christ are dead "outside the gate" of the city (Hebrews 13:12). The Hebrew Day of Atonement called for two goats to be offered during the ritual; one goat for a blood offering and the other as the scapegoat offering. Israel's sins were laid upon the scapegoat and expelled from the camp; the blood offering goat was sacrificed, the blood offered, and the body burned "outside the gate." (Leviticus 16:20-22).

3. He was raised for others. There are two dead people in this Luke 7:11-15 story; the boy and his widowed mother. The boy was physically dead. The mother was emotionally and spiritually dead. Notice that Jesus "felt compassion for her" (v. 13). Jesus raised the dead son for the sake of his mother. So, too, God the Father gave us His only begotten Son for the sake of others. "God so loved us" (John 3:16). The Apostle Paul described it this way: "God demonstrates his own love for us in this: While we were still sinners, Christ died for us" (Romans 5:8).

4. He was offered with a command. When Jesus raised the boy from the dead by the word of His power, He gave him back to his mother with this command (to the mother) - "Do not weep." This word 'weep' means more than tears; it speaks of mourning, lamenting, despairing, and giving up. Why should the mother not weep? This is the key: "Jesus gave him to his mother." To follow through fully with the type: "Do not mourn, God has raised His Son from the dead and given Him to us!"

Principle: The only anecdote against despair during a trying time-- including those occasions when our prayers seemingly go unanswered --is the growing comprehension of what God has already done for us in giving to us His resurrected Son.

"What then shall we say to these things? If God is for us, who is against us? He who did not spare His own Son, but delivered Him over for us all, how will He not also with Him freely give us all things? But in everything we overwhelmingly conquer through Him who loved us. For I am convinced that neither death, nor life, nor angels, nor principalities, nor things present, nor things to come, nor powers, nor height, nor depth, nor any other created thing, will be able to separate us from the love of God which is in Christ Jesus our Lord" (Romans 8:31-32; 37-39).

"But God, begin rich in mercy, because of His great love with which He loved us - even when we were dead in trespasses and sins ... raised us up with His Son and seated us with Him in heavenly places, so that in the ages to come He might show us the surpasses riches of His grace in His kindness toward us." (Ephesians 2:4-7).

Application

a. The greatest riches in my life are vertical, not horizontal. When I receive, comprehend, and enjoy the love of God for me in Christ Jesus, I no longer need or depend on the love of people in this life. So, even if those I love are gone (or turn against me) I rest in the love of Him who loves me eternally.

d. To the degree I lack comprehension of the riches of God's kindness, favor, and love for me in Christ Jesus I will be tempted to measure God's love, favor and kindness for me by whether or not God always answers my prayers the way I ask rather than rejoicing in what He has already done for me.

Chapter 27: Jesus Is the "New Israel" in God's New Agreement

Orthodox Jews and evangelical Christians have very little in common. The English usage of the adjective Judeo-Christian may make a person think that evangelicalism and Orthodox Judaism are similar. We really aren't. Admittedly, Judeo-Christian sounds more pleasant to the ears than Islamic-Christian to most American Christians, but there's about as much in common between religious Muslims and evangelicals as there is between religious Jews and evangelicals.

Yet, for many wrong reasons, some Christians believe it is "of God" to support Jewish attempts to extricate Muslims from Jerusalem, tear down the Dome of the Rock - a major Islamic shrine - in order to rebuild the Jewish Temple, re-institute Old Covenant blood sacrifices, and re-establish Old Covenant Festivals outlined in The Law (the five books of Moses).

I don't get it.

"Kiss the Son..." (Psalm 2:12) is the instruction of God for all peoples during these New Covenant times, both Jew and Gentile. It matters not if you are born in the land of Israel, a Muslim land, a secular land, or even a so-called "Christian" land, every single human is instructed by God to embrace Jesus Christ. To come to Christ by faith, and to declare "I have no righteousness except Him" is the essence of "good news," and it is the only way by which anyone will ever experience right standing with God and eternal blessings from God. Orthodox Jews oppose the proclamation of faith in the Person and work Jesus Christ as much as Muslims do.

For evangelicals to support the re-building of a Jewish Temple, the re-instituting of Jewish institutional sacrifices, and the re-establishing of Jewish annual Festivals -- all of which Jesus Christ caused to disappear (Hebrews 8:13) -- strikes me as anti-Christ.

God established a New Covenant (agreement) with the world through the obedience of His Son. The Old Covenant was made with one nation (Israel) and is now gone (disappeared). Whereas in the Old Covenant, the nation of Israel experienced God's blessings through their obedience to the Law, as well as God's wrath for their disobedience to the Law, in the New Covenant God's blessings are only received through not being ashamed of "the Christ of God" (Luke 9:20) and putting one's trust in Him.

This is why our obedience to God in the New Covenant is called "the obedience of faith" (Romans 16:26). We believe in Jesus Christ, embrace Him, refuse to be ashamed of Him, and claim we have no righteousness of our own, but only that righteousness which is found in Him.

That's why evangelicals who spend their time attempting to explain why it's necessary for Jews to re-institute the rituals of Old Covenant, constantly promoting the religion of Orthodox Judaism -- while at the same time denigrating orthodox Islam -- may have completely missed the beauty of Jesus Christ and the good news (i.e. "the gospel").

Jesus Christ is the New Israel

Most evangelicals read the New Testament and come across the phrase "the last days" and think it has to do with "the last days" of this world. Not true. The New Testament writers, all of whom were Jews, wrote of "the last days" of the Old Covenant! God was bringing to an end the covenant He made with national Israel. Through His Son, God was launching a New Agreement (Covenant) with the world (Hebrews 8:13). The Twelve original Disciples of

Christ knew they were in "the last days" of the Old Covenant, and this is why the Apostle John wrote in I John 2:18 that he was indeed living in "the last hour." Peter, when preaching on the day of Pentecost, quoted the prophet Joel and said Joel's words about "the last days" were then (in Peter's day) being fulfilled (Acts 2:17).

Other passages like Hebrews 1:1–2 say the early disciples were living in "the last days," and that the "consummation of the ages" was "now" (i.e. during the time of the early disciples - see Hebrews 9:26). Paul said the early Jewish followers of Christ were the people "upon whom the ends of the ages have come" (I Corinthians 10:11). The New Testament books were written prior to the collapse of Old Covenant Jewish worship (A.D. 70), and the early followers of Jesus - most of whom were Jewish - were prepared by Christ to anticipate the destruction of their Jewish way of worship "in the last days."

In A.D. 70 God brought the Romans to Jerusalem to destroy the Jewish Temple, end the blood sacrifices, and scatter the Jews, similar to the way He brought the Assyrians to Israel in 722 B.C. to end the northern kingdom of Israel, destroy the false idols they'd built in the groves, and scatter the ten northern tribes. The judgment of God wrought in A.D. 70 was also similar to the manner in which He brought an end to Temple worship and the desolation of Jerusalem in 586 B.C. through the army of the Babylonians. Believing God ended the Old Covenant age A.D. 70 doesn't preclude a belief that Jesus Christ is returning one day to raise the dead, judge the wicked, give His followers the rewards He has earned for them (i.e. "we are co-heirs with Christ"), and usher in eternity - all of which I believe. But what a proper understanding of the New Testament "last days" will do for you is help you put more of an emphasis on the Person and work of Jesus Christ and His Kingdom now rather than a nation whose covenant with God (the Old Covenant) has disappeared.

I support "national Israel" today because they are the closest thing to a democracy in the totalitarian despotism of the Middle East. I, like you, watch the news and feel sympathy and support for Israel because of the despotic enemies that surround them. However, to support "national Israel" because of a belief that God desires the re-establishment of an Old Covenant agreement with Israel is - forgive my expression - to spit in the face of Jesus, the Christ of God.

Jesus is the new Israel in the eternal New Agreement that God has made with the world. God is now only concerned with whether or not people everywhere embrace His Son. That's why you can talk about your religion (i.e. "How you serve God, worship God, obey God") and the world will leave you alone. But the moment you begin to talk about Jesus Christ, all hell breaks loose.

Jesus is the Christ of God, and even the demons of hell know you must embrace Him or face the wrath of God. When you promote national Israel over the New Israel (Jesus Christ), you are no different in your religion than any other anti-Christ religion. Faith that saves is Christo-centric. Saving faith is "Christ-centered" and not Old Covenant national Israel-centered.

"This Is My Son, in Whom I Am Well Pleased"

Let me show you how Jesus is the fulfillment of the Law and the new Israel in the new, eternal agreement that God has made with the world.

After Jesus was born in Bethlehem, his parents took Him to Egypt to avoid the murderous plot of King Herod. Later, Jesus left Egypt with Joseph and Mary and settled in Nazareth. When Matthew recounts how Jesus was "called out of Egypt" (Matthew 2:15), he says that Christ coming out of Egypt fulfills the statement of Hosea 11:1 - "Out of Egypt I have called My Son."

Wait a minute! That Hosea 11:1 passage says:

"When Israel was a child, I loved him, and out of Egypt I called my son."

But the gospel writer (Matthew) says that this statement from Hosea is fulfilled in the life of Jesus Christ. In other words, Jesus becomes the new Israel in the New Covenant. Unlike Old Covenant Israel, Jesus fulfills the Law - every jot and tittle of it! There are some evangelicals who believe that "the church" has replaced Israel in the New Covenant. Not so. Jesus is the new Israel.

Notice how the life of Jesus as the new Israel parallels the life of Old Covenant national Israel.

1. The King of Kings was born in Bethlehem, the very place where King David was crowned King of Israel during Old Covenant days.

2. After Jesus was born, He went to Egypt, just as national Israel fled to Egypt during Old Covenant days to avoid death (see Genesis 46:8).

3. Both national Israel and the new Israel (Jesus Christ) were "called out of Egypt" (Hosea 11:1).

4. God gave the Law during the Old Covenant on a mountain (Sinai) through Moses; and He gave the new Law on a mountain through His Son (i.e. "The Sermon on the Mount").

5. God told Peter, James and John to ignore Moses and Elijah, the great Law-giver and prophet of the Old Covenant, and to listen to "My beloved Son!" (*akoute auton* - "Hear Him"!"). Because HE is the Christ of God. We are to listen to Him alone! (see Luke 9:28-36).

6. National Israel has a history of disobedience to God and failure to meet the conditions of the Old Covenant. The new Israel, Jesus Christ, fulfilled every "jot and tittle" of the Law (Matthew 5:18).

7. Since the Law promised "blessings" from God for full obedience, and punishment for disobedience to the Law, national Israel experienced punishments from God throughout the duration of the Old Covenant (ending in AD 70). However, Jesus experienced

and felt the full pleasure of His father ("this is my beloved Son in whom I am well pleased") because of His perfect obedience.

8. Before Jesus entered into His public ministry of mercy and grace, He endured 40 days in the wilderness; so too, before national Israel entered into Canaan, they spent 40 years in the wilderness.

9. Jesus Christ was baptized at the very location (Betharaba) national Israel crossed the Jordan to enter Canaan

10. Jesus is the fulfillment of the Law's Festivals (born at Tabernacles, died at Passover, in the tomb during Unleavened Bread, raised on the Feast of First Fruits, and sending the Comforter at Pentecost, etc...).

Because Jesus perfectly fulfilled the Law in His perfect obedience, and passively fulfilled the Law in His substitutionary death (i.e. He paid the Law's penalty for sin), the good news is that whoever forsakes trust in their personal obedience and places their faith in the performance and work of Jesus Christ, the gift given to them is life -- real life that lasts forever -- which includes God's forgiveness of every sin, the crediting of Christ's perfect righteousness to my account (i.e. "God sees no sin in His people"), and eternal rewards for Christ's performance ("the meek will inherit the earth when the curse is fully reversed").

In this New Covenant time period, we are fully blessed by God, totally pleasing to God, and the eternally loved, adopted, and rewarded sons of God (by adoption) because of the obedience of Jesus Christ (not our own) and our faith in Him! As it is written:

But whatever was to my profit (as an orthodox, religious Jew) I now consider loss for the sake of Christ. What is more, I consider everything a loss compared to the surpassing greatness of knowing Christ Jesus my Lord, for whose sake I have lost all things. I consider them rubbish, that I may gain Christ and be found in him, not having a righteousness of my own that comes from the Law, but that which is through faith in Christ--the righteousness that comes from God and is by faith. I want to know Christ (Philippians 3:7-11).

In Jesus Christ We Have True Rest

Before you get all caught up in the questions of how people should treat modern, national Israel, may I suggest that God is only interested in how you treat the new Israel - His Son, the "Christ of God"? Christ fulfilled the Law whereas national Israel failed the Law, Christ is pleasing to God for His perfect obedience whereas national Israel experienced punishment from God for their persistent disobedience; Christ is "the Way, the Truth and the Life" for all those who put their faith in Him (i.e. "the obedience of faith," Romans 16:26), whereas national Israel has gone down a path "that seemed right to man, but the end thereof is the way of death" (Proverbs 14:12).

I believe any evangelical more concerned with one's treatment of national Israel than one's trust in the new Israel, Jesus Christ, is doing a disservice to the Kingdom of God and missing the Gospel itself by mixing and confusing an Old Covenant, replaced by a New Covenant inaugurated by the performance of the New Israel (Jesus Christ). I close with the words of the brilliant John Owen on why an understanding of the New Covenant and its corresponding freedom to those who embrace the New Israel (Jesus Christ) will revolutionize one's life and worship:

Foe "where the Spirit of the Lord is, there is liberty;" namely, to serve God, "not in the oldness of the letter, but in the newness of the Spirit."... And we may briefly consider wherein this deliverance and liberty by the New Covenant does consist, which it does in the following things:—

a. In our freedom from the commanding power of the law, as to sinless, perfect obedience, in order to obtain righteousness and justification before God.

b. In our freedom from the condemning power of the law, and the sanction of it in the curse. This being undergone and answered by Him who was "made a curse for us," we are freed from it, Rom. 7:6; Gal. 3:13, 14.

c. In our freedom from conscience (Heb. 10:2) —that is, freedom from the conscience disquieting, perplexing, and condemning our persons; the hearts of all that believe being "sprinkled from an evil conscience" by the blood of Jesus Christ.

d. In our freedom from the whole system of Musical worship, in all the rites, and ceremonies, and ordinances of it; which what a burden it was the apostles do declare…

e. From all the laws of men in things appertaining unto the worship of God, 1 Cor. 7:23.

And by all these, and the like instances of spiritual liberty, does the gospel free believers from that "spirit of bondage unto fear," which was administered under the Old Covenant.

Next time you experience a "spirit of fear" about the world's future, your personal failures, or the possibility of the loss of God's favor, you might check upon which Israel you are relying - the Old Israel which induces "a bondage unto fear" or the New Israel which brings life, liberty, and real happiness.

Action

I will spend more time learning about the love of God for me in what He has already done for me through His Son than I will worry about what God will do for me in the future through meeting a temporal need I have.

Conclusion:

Nain is a city in Israel that still exists. It's just to the southwest of Mt. Tabor in the Galilee region of Israel. The modernized spelling of Nain has switched to Nein. I've been there a few times on my trips to Israel, and I never pass through without thinking of "the widow of Nain" and what her story declares about God's compassion and love for me in giving me His Son.

Nein in German means "No."

If I am praying for God to do something miraculous in my life, but the circumstances play out in such a way that God seems to say "Nein" to my request, I want to remember the widow of "Nein" and learn to "weep not" because God has already given to me His Son. If indeed, I am able by God's grace to remember this principle, I will be able to say with all the saints...

"I love Nein"

Chapter 28: The New Covenant Creates an "Ability to Respond" rather than Greater Responsibility

If I had a nickel for every time I heard someone say, "I just need my husband held accountable to the responsibilities he has as a husband, father, and spiritual leader in my home," I think I would be a very rich man. For some reason "responsibility" is a very big word among evangelicals, particularly among those who seem disappointed with the state of affairs with others they love. Paul Tripp points out in his marriage series "What Did You Expect" that the problem within a marriage is a "problem within me."

However, very few people who seek my counsel for their marriage come with the attitude, "Pastor, I have a problem in me. A heart problem. I need some wisdom, help and encouragement." Usually, the conversation begins with the problems in one's spouse and a statement, "I just need help holding my spouse accountable to do what he is supposed to be done in our marriage."

My friend Paul Young recently wrote an insightful post that needs, in my opinion, wide circulation. Paul loves words, particular since the Word created the universe with one. Paul believes that words convey truth and have inherent power. He points out that there is a particular word not found in the Bible. It is not listed in Vines Expository Dictionary of New Testament Words, Tyndale Publisher's The Word Study Concordance (based on Strong's Concordance) and Geoffrey Bromley's 1,356 page Theological Dictionary of the New Testament, or the massive ten volume set of Gerhard Kittel's Theological Dictionary of the New Testament.

The word is responsibility.

It doesn't appear one time in the Bible. Nor do any of its derivations, including the word responsible. Hmm. How does this apply to those of us who know Jesus and are in love relationships with other people?

Paul writes:

"Instead of responsibility, the Bible chooses to focus on another action: the ability to respond.

This is entirely different. Responsibility is as set of expectations enforced from the outside. It's a law or code of behavior and often used to define a good person and communicate shame for poor performance.

But a response arises from within. It is dynamic and relational. A responsive person may or may not give, but a responsible person is supposed to give. Because of who we are as human beings indwelt by Jesus (John 14:20), we have an ability to respond, not a responsibility. This has massive implications and is implicitly an invitation to adventures in living.

Remember that today. Your call is not a responsibility. It is your willing and joyful response.

If people could ever stop considering responsibility as something God ordains in love relationships, and instead focused on "my ability to respond," I believe marriages, families, churches, and every other covenant relationship would be transformed.

Chapter 29: It's Worth Your Time and Effort to Know Why You Believe What You Believe

If there is anything worse than dogmatic, authoritarian churches where members are told what to believe and punished for questioning leaders, it is vapid churches where members are given nothing to believe and participate for the sake of being hip and cool.

Whereas the former churches ultimately fail because the Information Age launches church members into the stratosphere of interaction with scholars who give cogent arguments for opposing views and then leads them to eventually revolt against insecure authoritarians who blanche in the face of disagreement, the latter churches ultimately fail because members are never taught to value truth in the first place and shrug their shoulders and say, "What's the big deal?"

I've written extensively about authoritarian church leaders who squelch disagreement, but little has been said about theologically uninspiring leaders who are unable to teach people God's word.

No more. There is a rising sense within me that church light is more dangerous than church might. Those crushed by the abuse of church leaders who see themselves as God's vicars on earth are in need of our mercy and support, but those who are enmeshed in church light are also in need of an awakening. The former abuse is overt and painful; the latter abuse is subtle and sweet. In the end, the effects on church members are the same.

God's people ought to be able to articulate the reasons for the hope within them. The ability of church members to articulate the essential differences between egalitarianism and complementarianism, the different world views of dispensational premillennialists over and against partial preterists, the reasons why some believe the Old Covenant laws of Israel are abolished versus some who believe all laws in the covenants--both Old and New--remain in effect forever, as well as members being able to articulate for themselves other theological differences, should be not just the dream of pastors, it should be our goal.

For example, there's no way for Christians to explain the basis for believing the dietary laws of Israel are abolished unless those same Christians read and learn the books of Leviticus and Hebrews and then see how Scripture specifically teaches the person and work of Jesus Christ is foreshadowed in the dietary laws--every jot and tittle of them--and that Christ through His life, death and resurrection for sinners has made these Old Covenant law "obsolete" and causes them to "disappear" (Hebrews 8:13).

In addition, until Christians know the book of Daniel, they will never be able to explain how the prophet Daniel was given a vision foretelling the coming of the Messiah and His Kingdom, which would crush every earthly kingdom (Daniel 2:44) including Israel's, but that he was to seal up the "scroll of his book" because the time was 'far away' (Daniel 12:4). Unless people read Revelation for themselves and see that John's scroll was "not to be sealed because the time is near" (Revelation 22:10), they might never realize that Daniel's prophecy was fulfilled when Christ rose from the dead to inaugurate His eternal kingdom and then He waited forty years to utterly destroy Jerusalem and the Old Covenant kingdom of His people (the Jews) in righteous judgment.

Of course, the dispensational premillennialist would say that the kingdom of God has not YET been inaugurated, and unless Christians learn to understand the differences in eschatology, they will never be able to articulate why they believe what they believe about the future. Christians enmeshed in church light will never know the differences, much less what they believe, and struggle with understanding why they should care.

The goal of every pastor is not that every Christian in the church believes the same thing on tertiary issues of Scripture, but that every Christian in the church knows the arguments of both sides of an issue and is able to articulate why he or she believes what is believed! Peter writes,

"But sanctify the Lord God in your hearts, and be ready always to give an answer to every man who asketh you a reason for the hope that is in you" (I Peter 3:15).

It seems Peter is saying one's confidence in the Lord is strengthened when one is able to articulate the reason for the hope that is within. To be able to articulate your beliefs as a Christian in areas of marriage, eschatology, church governance, New Covenant and Old Covenant theology, the person and work of Christ, and hundreds of other important issues from Scripture is the sign that you are maturing and growing in your faith relationship with God.

I would rather have a church member who is a complementarian, dispensational, Old Covenant Presbyterian, believer in male authority and is able to articulate what he believes from his interpretation of the Scripture (though I strongly disagree with him), than I would a member who cares nothing for the truth of Scripture and revels in church light and vapid preachers who "coach" instead of biblically literate preachers who teach the Bible.

There is an official organization called Church Lite. It is composed of atheists, agnostics, and all those who deny the existence of God. Their statement of faith:

"We remove all of the guilt over offending imaginary beings and of enjoying life ("bad guilt") while retaining most of the guilt over harming others ("good guilt") and some guilt over privilege (in the form of concern over the plight of the less fortunate) (not present in all competing churches)."

Sadly, evangelical church lights share similarities with atheistic church lites. Both have lost sight of the person and work of Jesus Christ in removing guilt by Himself.

Chapter 30: Giving Grace under the New Covenant to Sinners Coming Out of the Closet

I received my Sports Illustrated this week and on the front cover was a picture of NBA basketball player Jason Collins and the big bold words Jason Comes Out in the article itself. Jason announced to the world that he is attracted to same-sex sexual relationships. He said it was time to stop hiding in the proverbial closet, come out, and "live truthfully." Good for Jason. He is honest about his desires to have sexual relations with men. Some might say, "No, he is only speaking about his sexual orientation. He is attracted to men." I respond, "Attracted in what sense?

"Many of us (men) are attracted to other men in friendship, and attracted to men in relationship, and attracted to men in companionship. Jason is coming out and declaring his attraction to having sex with men--or possibly a man--and he is being honest about it. Again, good for him. Jason says, "Greater openness and honesty promotes increased understanding, respect and acceptance." I agree with you Jason.

For example, I have a friend who is sexually attracted to exposing himself to women. He hid his desires--and behavior--for many, many years. When he finally came out of the closet with his wife, family and friends (including me), we began to understand him better. My friend will tell you he has never been loved and accepted by anyone the way he was when I went down to the police station and hugged him and told him I loved him and was there for him. I walked with him through the hurtful process of coming out of the closet and confessing to his sexual attraction to seeing the looks on women's faces when he exposed himself. I stood with him when the police mocked him. I stood with him when the judge sentenced him.

Many people were disgusted with him because of his sexual orientation and his sexual actions. Not me. I accepted him, appreciated his honesty, and stood by him. His honesty with me helped me understand why he was attracted to exposing himself to women. I agree with Jason Collins: "Greater openness and honesty promotes understanding, respect and acceptance" -- at least with me.

I have another couple of friends who are sexually attracted to women who are not their wives, and on more than one occasion have acted out on those attractions. I would consider them two of my best friends. When they came out of the closet many years ago regarding their sexual orientations, I stood beside them, respected them and accepted them. Both confess to others that I helped save their lives, and both confess that their sexual orientations have not changed, only that they are beginning to understand the beauty of having sex with the person to whom God has given to them in the covenant of marriage. In one case, a marriage was saved; in another, a marriage was not. My love for both men is present even when some in their own families turned against them. Again, I agree with Jason Collins: "Greater openness and honesty promotes understanding, respect and acceptance."

I have another friend who was arrested for solicitation of sex from a minor. He confesses to being oriented toward having a desire for sex with young people, particularly those who are in the age range of 10 to 12. He went to prison for his crime. He will tell you that I have stood with him, respected him and accepted him. Everywhere he goes in our church he must be announced as a "child predator." We know that many say a child predator is not a human being, but God forbid those words ever come from my mouth.

When my friend came out of the closet several years ago, I accepted him, respected him and understood him better, even as we encouraged the courts to sentence him for his crimes. I agree with Jason Collins that "greater openness and honesty" promotes better relationships. My friend will tell you he has never been loved like I have loved him--by anyone.

I know some of you are saying, "Wait a minute! How can you compare the sexual orientations of a homosexual or an adulterer with those who expose their genitalia to others, or a child predator! The first two involve consenting adults! The latter two involve crimes perpetrated against the non-consenting or children!" I respond: Do you not know history? The Roman emperors during the Roman Empire declared sex between men and young boys both legal and beneficial.

The Greeks considered men exposing themselves to women a sign of masculinity and patriarchal power. Just because sex with children goes against your sense of morality or exposing yourself to non-consenting women goes against your sense of morality, it doesn't mean that it goes against everyone else's sense of morality. Cultures change. As my friend John Blanchard says, "The new morality is actually old immorality."

The American culture is changing. It used to be that same-sex sexual conduct was illegal in America, punishable by a prison sentence. It used to be that adultery was illegal in America, punishable by a prison sentence. Some people in America are pushing to legalize sex with children, just as the ancient Romans did, because how can you call an act of love with a child wrong?

Here's the deal. I agree with Jason Collins: "We need more honesty." We need more people to continue to come out of the closet. We need more people to be transparent about their struggles with sexual orientation and their struggles in acting out. We need to commend Jason Collins--and anyone else for that matter--for coming out of the closet and making known their sexual orientation. And, we need to love them, respect them and accept them--as immoral people in need of God's grace.

This is the message of Christ. He is in love with sinners. He came for sinners, not the righteous, and until a homosexual, adulterer, sexual lover of children, or any other sexually immoral person can be honest and call their desires and actions sinful, there is no hope for ever trusting Christ and receiving God's forgiveness and transformative power to change. The standard of human morality is set by revelation not by speculation. The Scripture is clear: "Or do you not know that wrongdoers will not inherit the kingdom of God? Do not be deceived: Neither the sexually immoral nor idolaters nor adulterers nor men who have sex with men nor thieves nor the greedy nor drunkards nor slanderers nor swindlers will inherit the kingdom of God" (I Corinthians 6:9-10).

All the friends mentioned above have come to Christ. Since becoming believers in Christ, all of their sinful orientations and desires have not disappeared. Coming out of the closet and admitting their orientation toward sexual immorality was a first step to finding grace. All of them have had sexually immoral desires since coming to faith in Christ, and most of them have been sexually immoral in conduct since coming to Christ. Yet, they continue to be honest about their struggles, and they call their acting out sexual immorality. They have been loved and accepted by me as I've walked them through the process of continued healing and change, and I will be with them to the end.

I close with profound words from C.S. Lewis on sexual immorality, words that I pray characterize my love, respect and acceptance toward those who come out of the closet and the truth I will tell them when they do:

"Our warped natures, the devils who tempt us, and all the contemporary propaganda for lust, combine to make us feel that the desires we are resisting are so 'natural,' so 'healthy, and so reasonable, that it is almost perverse and abnormal to resist them. Poster after poster, film after film, novel after novel, associate the idea of sexual indulgence with the ideas of health, normality, youth, frankness, and good humor. Now this association is a lie. Like all powerful lies, it is based on a truth--the truth . . . that sex in itself (apart from the excess and obsessions that have grown around it) is 'normal,' and 'healthy,' and all the rest of it.

The lie consists in the suggestion that any sexual act to which you are tempted is also healthy and normal. Now this, on any conceivable view, and quite apart from Christianity, must be nonsense. Surrender to all of our desires obviously leads to impotence, disease, jealousies, lies, concealment, and everything that is the reverse of good health, good humor, and frankness. For any happiness, even in this world, quite a lot of restraint is going to be necessary . . . For 'nature' (in the sense of natural desire) will have to be controlled anyway, unless you are going to ruin your whole life.

I want to make it as clear as I possibly can that the center of Christian morality is not here. If anyone thinks that Christians regard unchastity as the supreme vice, he is quite wrong.

The sins of the flesh are bad, but they are the least bad of all sins. All the worst pleasures are purely spiritual: the pleasure of putting other people in the wrong, of bossing and patronizing and spoiling sport, and backbiting; the pleasures of power, of hatred. For there are two things inside me, competing with the human self which I must try to become. They are the Animal self, and the Diabolical self. T

The Diabolical self is the worse of the two. That is why a cold self-righteous prig who goes regularly to church may be far nearer to hell than a prostitute. But, of course, it is better to be neither."

Chapter 31: The New Covenant Believer Rejoices in Being "Outside the Camp"

"Let us go to Him outside the camp, bearing His reproach" (Hebrews 13:13).

The sacrifices in the Old Testament foreshadowed the coming of the Messiah like a shadow protruding from a corner on a sunny day portends the coming of a person. The Old Covenant practice of sacrificing lambs, goats, and bulls foretell in picture form the coming of "the Lamb of God who takes away the sin of the world." The Day of Atonement (Yom Kippur) was the most important holiday on the Jewish calendar. It was called the Sabbath of Sabbaths by the Hebrews.

Two goats were brought into the camp for the Yom Kippur sacrifice. The first goat brought into the camp on the Day of Atonement was killed. The blood of this goat was sprinkled seven times before the altar, and then a basin of its blood was taken through the curtain into the holy of holies and sprinkled seven times before the Ark of the Covenant (Leviticus 16). Peace with God is foreshadowed through this Yom Kippur ritual, for "without the shedding of blood there is no forgiveness of sins" (Hebrews 9:22). Jesus Christ's blood "cleanses us from all sin" and through our faith in Christ we have peace with God (Romans 8:1). The body of this goat was taken by the priest outside the camp and burned.

The second goat, called the scapegoat, had a scarlet ribbon tied around its neck. The high priest would lay his hands on the head of the scapegoat and confess the sins of Israel. The scapegoat would then be taken by the priest outside the camp and lost in the desert.

The scapegoat foreshadows how Christ would bear the sins of His people and separate their sins from them "as far as the east is from the west." The Messiah was named Jesus because "He shall save His people from their sins" (Matthew 1:21).

God sees no sin in His people because our Scapegoat has carried them away. They are taken outside the camp and lost forever.

Outside the camp. This is an Old Covenant principle. Sin and shame are outside the camp in the Old Covenant. Lepers and the outcasts of Israel lived outside the camp. Outside the camp was an unclean place for unclean people. The priest who carried the body of the goat to be burned outside the camp had to go through purification rituals before he was even allowed back inside the camp (Leviticus 16:28). Nobody went outside the camp in the Old Covenant during Yom Kippur unless the Hebrews cast them out as unworthy, unwanted, and unwelcome.

Jesus Christ fulfilled the Law--"every jot and tittle"--and died for us outside the camp. It is a known historical fact that Jesus Christ was crucified, bearing our sin "outside the gate" of Jerusalem (Hebrews 13:12). "So, let us go to Him outside the camp, bearing His reproach" (Hebrews 13:13).
Whereas the Hebrew in the Old Covenant were never to go outside the gate, the writer of the New Testament book of Hebrews calls for us to "go to Him outside the gate."

The New Covenant turns the Old Covenant principle of "outside the camp" on its head. In the Old Covenant, sin and shame were outside the camp and no Hebrew dared go outside the camp. In the New Covenant, Christ died outside the gate and followers of Christ are called to "go to Him outside the camp, bearing His reproach."

What does this mean?

(1). A New Covenant believer is not afraid to call himself "the chief of sinners" (I Timothy 1:15). A church that does not understand the New Covenant and lives by Old Covenant principles points the finger at those "outside the camp" and considers them vile and horrible. Old Covenant churches have an "us vs. them" mentality. "Those people out there" are vile and wicked, but we who are "in the camp" are not. The truth is, when a sinner goes outside the camp to embrace Christ, bearing His reproach, he identifies himself as one of the least, the last, the little and the lost - the outcast.

(2). A New Covenant believer is more concerned with relationships than religion. "Let us go to Him outside the gate." Churches who have a camp mentality are designed to make life comfortable for those inside the camp. Songs are sung because those that are singing the songs enjoy others praising them for their voices. Messages are preached because those that are delivering the messages enjoy the accolades of the hearers. Programs and ministries are funded and staffed because those involved feel good about themselves for what they are doing.

Churches based on Old Covenant principles are more interested in people in the camp feeling good about themselves than they are identifying with the least, the last, the little and the lost outside the camp and taking them to Christ. I've said it before, but it's worth saying again, "The measure of greatness for any church is not how many it sits but how many it sends." Anything in a church that gives an "us vs. them" impression to the outside world is a church based on Old Covenant principles. The truth is, we ARE them; the only difference is we have come to Him.

(3). A New Covenant believer lives in freedom and pays little attention to what those in the camp think. When a sinner comes to faith in Christ, the truth of what Christ has done sets the sinner free. The full forgiveness from God and the immeasurable love of God causes the believer to live life in an abundant fashion. Rather than living in bondage to expectations, perceptions, and demands of others, the New Covenant believer follows the Spirit and lives in real freedom.

In addition, for the sinner who meets Christ outside the camp, there is no longer any desire to put roots down in any city, organization or camp that will not last (Hebrews 13:14). There is only a desire for "the city with foundations" whose Builder and Maker is God (Hebrews 11:10).

I am greatly encouraged from the Word of God to realize that my job is not to make people comfortable "in the camp" but to stretch us all to go "outside the camp" and identify with the least, the last, the little and the lost in order to lead them to the only One who takes away that which will truly destroy and gives to us that which we can eternally enjoy.

Chapter 32: Spirit Led Living Is the Only Way to Live in the New Covenant

Tim Keller published an article entitled Old Testament Law and the Charge of Inconsistency. In this article he writes, "I find it frustrating when I read or hear columnists, pundits, or journalists dismiss Christians as inconsistent because 'they pick and choose which of the rules in the Bible to obey.' What I hear most often is 'Christians ignore lots of Old Testament texts about not eating raw meat or pork or shellfish, not executing people for breaking the Sabbath, not wearing garments woven with two kinds of material and so on. Then they condemn homosexuality. Aren't you just picking and choosing what they want to believe from the Bible?'"

Keller goes on to show in the article how Jesus Christ calls both adultery and homosexuality contrary to God's design for men and women (Matthew 19:3-12). He then gives a 'short course on the relationship of the Old Testament to the New Testament.' Keller brilliantly shows 'the surpassing significance' of Christ, and how the Old Testament foreshadows the work of Jesus Christ--a work that Christ completely fulfilled--on behalf of sinners. He rightly shows that to continue abiding by the Old Covenant laws of ancient Judaism one would "deny the power of Christ's death on the cross!"

I could not agree more with Dr. Keller on this point. However, I believe Dr. Keller makes a major error when he writes, "the coming of Christ changed how we worship but not how we live."

Christ's Coming Changes Everything

The coming of Christ changes everything about the way we live. We are now people led by the Spirit, not people led by Law. We listen to the voice of Christ, and are no longer bound to ANY Law of the Old Covenant. The Temple laws, the dietary laws, the Sabbath laws, the circumcision laws, the gender laws, the tithing laws, the hierarchical laws of authority, and all other laws of ancient Israel have been 'annihilated' by the death and resurrection of His Son (see Hebrews 10:9).

The hermeneutic or interpretative principle that leads Christians to live differently than Old Testament Jews is foreshadowed in the transfiguration of Christ. Jesus went to a mountain with a few of His disciples, and while on top of the mountain, Jesus was transfigured by Jehovah. In other words, God changed Christ's appearance in the presence of Peter, James and John (Mark 9:2-9), and they caught a glimpse of the Eternal Lawgiver. Notice closely what happens next, as recorded by Mark in his gospel.

Mark writes that when the disciples saw Jesus transfigured, they became very afraid. Their fear was heightened when they saw the lawgiver of Israel (Moses) and the prophet of Israel (Elijah) suddenly standing next to the Eternal Lawgiver (Jesus the Anointed One). This amazing site transfixed the disciples. Peter, not knowing what to do or say, blurts out, "Teacher, it is good that we all are here. Let us make three tents: One for You, and one for Moses, and one for Elijah." (v.5).

Suddenly, the earth shook, a cloud descended and blanketed the mountain and the disciples fell on their faces in fear. A Voice spoke to the disciples saying, "This is my beloved Son; listen to Him!" When the cloud disappeared the disciples looked around and saw NOBODY BUT JESUS. Moses the ancient Lawgiver of Israel and Elijah, the ancient prophet of Israel were gone. God was saying, "Everything about the way you live is changing. Follow the direction of My Son." The original two words that form the last sentence of God's instructions to the disciples are "akoute auton" - Hear Him!

Christ Alone Is Our Authority

Christ's voice is the voice to which we listen. He supersedes the Old Covenant Law of Moses and the Old Covenant sayings of the prophets. Hear Him! The Old Covenant possessed a "fading glory" (II Corinthians 3:13) and has been destroyed. The New Covenant, signed and sealed by the blood of Christ, is far superior in nature and glory! It changes everything about how we live.

Whereas in the Old Covenant you looked to your obedience to Laws for your right standing with God, in the New Covenant, you look to Christ's obedience and by faith in Him you are "declared righteous" by God. Whereas in the Old Covenant you reaped the rewards of your personal obedience to the law ("If you do this... then I (Jehovah) will do this"), in the New Covenant, you reap all the rewards of the personal obedience of Another. As Paul says, "I have a righteousness of my own that does not come from my obedience to any law, but a righteousness that comes from God and is mine through faith" (Philippians 3:9). All of my hope and confidence in life is in Him. All of my hope and confidence is in Him! I love Him, and I listen to Him! He is my Master. I "akoute auton." I hear Him!

There is, however, a slight problem. Unlike the disciples that walked with Christ on earth, we can't see Christ visibly or hear Him audibly. We can't physically walk with Him, personally and audibly talk with Him, privately eat with Him, or publicly minister with Him--so how in the world do we "hear Him" since He's gone? Of course, we have the record of what He said to the disciples who came before us, and we study His words carefully. But Jesus gives us another answer to this question. Right before He left the disciples to "Go and prepare a place for those who love Him," He said something astonishing. "It is to your advantage that I go away, for if I do not go away, the Helper will not come to you. But if I go, I will send him to you . . . When the Spirit of truth comes, the Spirit will guide you . . ." (John 16:7-8, 13).

New Covenant believers must resist any imposition of religious laws that restrict the leadership and guidance of the Holy Spirit.

The New Covenant Is Christian Living at Its Finest

One of the best things we can do for others is to teach and model the New Covenant. The word "covenant" in Hebrew is [beriyth], and in Greek it is [diatheke], often translated "testament." Both original words literally mean "a promise or solemn oath" (See Genesis 26:3). We help others when they hear us teach, and they see us live, resting in God's solemn promise of faithful goodness toward us - regardless of our performance, obedience or commitment.

For Christians to understand this radical way of thinking and living, we must first understand that there two kinds of covenants that God enters into as described by Scripture. First, God has often entered into covenants that are based on a *mutual* agreement, so that God makes a promise to bless based upon certain requirements being met by the recipient of the promise. But there is a second kind of covenant or "promise" that God enters into, and fulfills, with no requirements or necessary stipulations from the recipient of the promise. This kind of covenant is called "an unconditional covenant." Unconditional covenants are entered into because of the mere grace of the promise maker.

Though there are several conditional covenants that God has made with His people throughout history as recorded in the Old Testament, there is one major conditional covenant, under which all other conditional covenants were made. The writer of Hebrews officially calls this covenant that God initiated with His people "The Old Covenant." God said, "If you will obey me . . . then I will bless you. If you disobey me, then I will curse you," and all Israel agreed. But the writer of Hebrews tells us that this covenant has been done away with and replaced with a "New Covenant" (Hebrews 9:15) between God and both Jews and Gentiles - all who will trust His

Son. This "New Covenant" is a "better" covenant with "better" promises; promises that are unconditional in nature.

A believer in Jesus Christ is the recipient of promises from God that are based on His mere grace, and have nothing to do with the performance or commitment of the participants. Simply "look to Christ and live." Unfortunately, many pastors do harm to their congregations by not understanding themselves the differences between the two covenants. A New Covenant preacher will tell God's people what God has done for us through His Son, our Savior Jesus Christ. New covenant messages and ministries will not be on "if you will . . . then God will . . . "but rather, "look what God has promised to do, and will do, for those who trust Him." It is to this ministry, with this message, that Jesus has called all minister to others the good news.

But our High Priest [Jesus Christ] has been given a ministry that is far superior to the ministry of those who serve under the old laws, for he is the one who guarantees for us a better covenant with God, based on better promises. If the first covenant had been faultless, there would have been no need for a second covenant to replace it. But God himself found fault with the old one when he said: "The day will come, says the Lord, when I will make a new covenant with the people of Israel and Judah..." (Heb. 8:6-8 NLT)

I was once asked why our church did not have an active "Promise Keepers" movement within it, and I responded that when the emphasis is on "The Promise Keeper," meaning God, then we would be involved. I have found that when ministries are built on the promises of man, they always tend to fail in the end.

However, it is not my desire to focus in this chapter on the specifics of how a ministry implements New Covenant teaching in terms of tithing, church attendance, and Christian commitment. There are plenty of websites that delve into this, including several articles by my own father, Paul Burleson.

The purpose of this particular chapter is to simply show that in the New Covenant there is a particular characteristic that defines God's people. We are not defined by our "obedience to any law" such as the law of Sabbath keeping, or the law of sacrifice, or the law of Temple worship, or the law of abstinence, or any other Old Covenant law, church law, or man-made law. Rather, we are defined as a people by our desire to solely and completely fulfill one law - the law from Jesus Christ Himself, called "the Royal Law of Love."

Jesus calls this Royal Law His "new commandment" (John 13:39). It is "new" in that it is a "new" commandment for the "new" man whose been given a "new" name and sings a "new" song as he lives a "new" life where all things are "new" (Rev. 21:5). It is this radical commandment to love one another - to boldly, liberally and continually love people - that is THE IDENTIFYING MARK of God's people. This does not mean that a New Covenant believer cannot be a person of strong convictions, but it does mean that love for people is to pervade all he or she does.

One of the best ways to measure whether or not we are living the Christian life to its fullest and it's finest is to measure whether our hearts are truly filled with love for people - people who disagree with us, people who are different than us, people who are a delight to us. Do we rejoice when others are blessed? Are we glad when others succeed? Do we do what we do because we love?

These are questions I ask myself almost daily.

Chapter 33: The New Covenant Leads Us to Rest and to Say "There's No Other Way"

When anyone receives a personal letter (or email), the mind subconsciously asks the question, "What is the writer's intent?" Response to personal communication is guided by our perception of the sender's reasons for writing.

If you believe, as I do, that the Bible is the inspired, written word from God to us, then we are wise to ask the questions:

(1). "What is God's intent in giving us His Word?" and
(2). "If it is correct that 'The chief end of man is to glorify God and enjoy Him forever,' then what does God's Word say about *how* we glorify and enjoy Him?"

When we correctly answer those two questions, we have discovered the general theme of God's Word.

I propose the overall, general theme of the Bible--both Old and New Testaments--is God's expressed desire that His people rest in Him. "Come to Me all you who are weary and burdened and I will give you rest" (Matthew 11:28).

God's preeminent desire for His people is not that we work; not that we serve; not that we worship; not that we love; not that we forgive; not that we pray; not that we witness; and not even that we glorify Him. God's preeminent desire is that we rest in Him. Only after we find our rest in Him will we have the desire to serve, to worship, to love, to forgive, to pray, to witness and to glorify. If this concept were in the form of a principle, it would sound like this: Our rest in Him becomes our glory of Him.

Rest in the Old Testament

Rest is the theme of the Bible from the beginning. God created the universe, and then He rested. The Hebrew word translated "rest" in Genesis 2:2 is Shabbat, from which we get our English word Sabbath. God did not rest on the seventh day of creation because He was tired, for the Scripture says "The everlasting God, the Lord, the Creator of the ends of the earth, neither faints nor is weary" (Isaiah 4:28). God rested because His work of creation was a "complete and perfect" work, or as the King James translators put it - "very good." When God completes a perfect work that He performs, the appropriate response is rest.

When God chose the Jews as His people from among all the nations of the earth, He gave them a commandment to rest on the seventh day of the week (Leviticus 23:2-3). The weekly Sabbath rest from physical work was to be a picture of God's people resting in Him. Any Hebrew who violated the weekly Sabbath rest was put to death (Numbers 15:32-36). This penalty may sound harsh to modern ears, but the punishment conveys God was either serious about the Sabbath itself or what the Sabbath ultimately pictured.

In addition to every weekly Sabbath rest, every seventh year became a year of agricultural rest (Heb. *shmita*) for the Hebrews and their land (see Leviticus 25:1-8). God's people could till, sow and harvest for six years, but they were to leave the ground fallow and rest from sowing and harvesting during the seventh year. God promised the Hebrews, "I will so order My blessing for you in the sixth year that it will bring forth the crop for three years" (Leviticus 25:21). God's people were to rest and trust Him--His provision, His promises and His faithfulness.

Finally, in addition to a weekly rest and a seventh year sabbatical land rest, after completing seven sevens of agricultural rest--that means 49 years--God commanded the Hebrews to celebrate another entire year of rest called the Jubilee Year (the 50th year). The Jubilee Year began the tenth day of the seventh month (Tishri) which was The Day of Atonement.

The Jews called The Day of Atonement "The Sabbath of Sabbaths" and of all the sacred days in Israel, commencement of Jubilee was most sacred (Leviticus 25:8-17). "This fiftieth year is sacred—it is a time of freedom and celebration when everyone will receive back their original property, and slaves will return home to their families" (Leviticus 25:10 NIV). During Jubilee, captives were to be set free, debts were to be forgiven, and the Hebrews were to rest in God's perfect provision for them. Rest, not work, was the predominate theme of the Law of God.

The Hebrews were taught that "The Law was only a shadow of the good things that are coming--not the reality themselves" (Hebrews 10:1). Just like seeing a shadow tells you that a real person is coming, so the Old Covenant Law, including the commandments to rest (Sabbath Laws), was a shadow that prefigured the One who would come and give real. eternal rest. The major consequence of sin is labor, "sweat work," and "thorns and thistles" in the harvest. Sin produces the opposite of rest, and the Law foreshadowed God's determination to wipe out the destructiveness of sin through the Anointed One (Messiah).

The problem with the Jews is that they not only violated the Law of God when it came to rest, they ultimately rejected the One whom the Law prefigured.

The Hebrews Refusal to Rest

Moses led God's people in an exodus from Egypt in 1491 B.C. Due to a lack of trust in God's faithfulness to fulfill His promise of bringing them safely into the Promised Land, Israel wandered for forty years in the desert. Again, the opposite of rest is restless, laborious wandering.

Finally, Joshua led the Hebrews in 1450 B.C. into the Promised Land. The Jews conquered and divided the lush land among their twelve tribes. Israel finally rested in God's abilities and not their own, and the walls of Jericho came tumbling down. When Israel became tempted again with the delusion of self-sufficiency, they labored on their own at Ai and lost the battle. God was teaching His people the principle of resting in Him even in time of conflict.

After taking possession of Canaan, the Israelites initially obeyed God's Sabbath laws regarding rest. But as time passed, the Hebrews began looking around at other nations, and they began to beg God for a king to rule over them. It looked easier from their perspective to trust in a monarchy rather than to rest in a theocracy. "Set a king over us like all the nations who are around us" (Deuteronomy 17:14). The Apostle Paul says, "When Israel asked for a king, God gave them Saul the son of Kish, a man of the tribe of Benjamin, for forty years" (Acts 13:21).

Bishop Ussher's chronology places Saul's coronation as king of Israel in 1095 B.C. Though I believe Saul was crowned King 40 years after this, the year 1095 is important. Samuel is the last prophet. Israel is finally becoming settled as a nation. It's time for Israel plant their crops and follow the Law of God. Every seventh year they are to rest. Bishop Usher points out that the crowning of Saul as king of Israel marks the exact year the Hebrew people stopped observing Sabbath rest. Institutional systems designed to give people security without promoting rest in God's grace – regardless of whether the system is corporate, political, or religious in nature – create a sense of self-sufficiency within people.

For 490 years after 1095 B.C., God's people refused to keep the seventh year agricultural rest commandment. The reason for Israel's refusal ito rest is not given, but it couldn't have been because of ignorance. The Law of God was clear, and God's people clearly knew the Law. In spite of God's expressed command that they rest in Him on various Sabbaths, the Hebrew people began tilling, sowing, and harvesting crops during the seventh year. Those 490 Shabbat forsaking years (from 1095 B.C. to 605 B.C.) meant the seventh year agricultural land rest was not kept by Israel seventy times (70 x 7 years equals 490 years). When God initially gave Israel the Law on Mt. Sinai, He told the people what would happen if they refused to observe the Sabbaths.

"I will lay waste your cities as well and will make your sanctuaries desolate...I will scatter you among the nations and will draw out a sword after you, as your land becomes desolate and your cities become wasted. Then the land will enjoy its Sabbaths all the days of desolation while you are in your enemies land; then the land will rest and enjoy its Sabbaths. All the days of its desolation it will observe the rest which it did not observe on your Sabbaths, while you were living on it" (Leviticus 26:31-35).

490 years after Israel stopped practicing Sabbath rest, God raised up Nebuchadnezzar II of Babylon to punish Israel. The year was 605 B.C. It was King Nebuchadnezzar's first year on the throne. His father, King Nabopolassar, had defeated the Assyrians four years earlier (609 B.C.), leading Babylon to become the world's second great empire (Assyria had been the world's first). In 605 B.C. King Nabopolassar abdicated the Babylonian throne and gave it to his son Nebuchadnezzar II. King Nebuchadnezzar led his army to Jerusalem to make war against the Hebrews. God's judgment of Israel had begun.

God used King Nebuchadnezzar to fulfill the promise He made to Israel in Leviticus 26:31-35, a promise of judgment via desolation and destruction if the Hebrews violated God's Law regarding rest. Nebuchadnezzar came against Jerusalem in 605 B.C., the first of what would eventually be three Babylonian attacks on the Jewish capital city (605 B.C.; 597 B.C.; and 587 B.C.) In the first siege, Nebuchadnezzar captured Daniel and a handful of other young Hebrew men and took them back to Babylon to serve in his court (see Daniel 1). The prophet Daniel would never again return to Israel.

King Nebuchadnezzar came back to Jerusalem in 587 B.C. for his third and final attack against the capital city of the Jews. He laid siege to the city for several months and eventually succeeded in

586 B.C. in demolishing the Hebrew Temple and the city of Jerusalem. Nebuchadnezzar carried away the rest of the Jews into Babylon.

586 B.C. marks the beginning of what is commonly called the Babylonian Captivity for the Jews. Israel experienced God's promised judgment for their violations of Sabbath Law. Understanding the reason for the Babylonian captivity crystallizes one's understanding of the Old Testament, particularly the Law and the Prophets and the historical narratives, for all these writings deal with Israel's refusal to rest in God, as well as God's promised judgment on Israel for their violations of His command to rest.

70 Years of Judgment for Babylon and for Israel

The number 70 is the number of years associated with God's judgment upon both Babylon and Israel. God promised He would raise up Babylon to desolate Israel for their sin, but He would only allow Babylon 70 years as a world power before He would make them become servants of other nations and free His people from their captivity. Throughout Scripture, God orchestrates pagan nations to accomplish His purpose, but then punishes those same nations for their free-will rebellion against Him. A sovereign God is able to orchestrate all events, even acts of sin which He never authors or originates, for ultimately good purposes.

This is what the LORD says: 'When seventy years are completed for Babylon, I will visit you (My people) and fulfill my good word to you...' (Jeremiah 29:10).

"'When seventy years are completed I will punish the king of Babylon and that nation,' declares the Lord, 'for their iniquity...I will bring upon Babylon all My words which I have pronounced against it, all that is written in this book which Jeremiah has prophesied against all the nations. For many nations and great kings will make slaves of them, even them; and I will recompense them according to their deeds and according to the work of their hands.'" (Jeremiah 25:12-14).

Babylon became a world power when it defeated Assyria in 609 B.C., but 70 years later, in 539 B.C., just as God promised, God brought the Babylonian kingdom to an end. God used the Medes and the Persians and their combined armies under the leadership of the remarkable Cyrus the Great, King of Persia, to defeat the mighty Babylonians. Cyrus and his Persian engineers diverted the river running underneath the walls of Babylon and dried up the river bed.

The Medo-Persian army then snuck into the walled city of Babylon, breaching the impenetrable walls of Babylon, crawling on their bellies underneath the walls. The very night the Persians invaded Babylon, King Belshazzar and his 1,000 Babylonian princes were drinking themselves into a drunken stupor inside the Palace Walls of the Great Hall (see Daniel 5). The city of Babylon, fortified by walls people consider to be one of the 7 Wonders of the Ancient World, fell to King Cyrus and the Medo-Persian army during one night of fighting.

The 70 years of Babylonian self-sufficiency were up (609 B.C. to 539 B.C.). The Hebrew prophecies of God's judgment against Babylon, prophecies given decades before Babylon's actual fall, are gripping portrayals of what happens to any person or country of people, whether Hebrew or not, who deem themselves sufficient and the Creator God unnecessary (see Isaiah 13:9-13 as an example of a prophecy predicting the downfall of Babylon).

God also judged His people, the Hebrews, with 70 years of desolation for their self-sufficiency refusal to rest in God. Of all the nations on the earth, Israel should have known better. In the last chapter of Chronicles, the chronicler describes the reason for 70 years of Hebrew desolation and exile at the hands of the Babylonians:"The land (of Israel) enjoyed its Sabbath rests; all the time of its desolation it rested until the seventy years were completed in fulfillment of the word of the Lord spoken by Jeremiah." (2 Chronicles 36:21).

Israel's punishment at the hands of the Babylonians was to be 70 years to make up for the 70 Sabbatical years of agricultural rest that Israel refused to keep beginning with Saul's anointing as king (1095 B.C.) and ending with Nebuchadnezzar's first appearance at Jerusalem (605 B.C.).

Some believe this judgment of 70 years of desolation for the land of Israel began in 609 B.C. In that year, King Josiah, one of the good kings of Israel's southern kingdom, refused the Egyptians permission to pass through Judah on their way to help the Assyrians fight their losing battle against the Babylonians. The Egyptian pharaoh was so furious with Josiah's refusal of safe passage that he led the Egyptian army to war against the Hebrews in what is called the Battle of Megiddo.

King Josiah was killed by the Egyptian Pharaoh Necho at that battle (see II Kings 23:29-30). God's judgment on Israel through the new world power of Babylon had begun. If the clock for the 70 years of promised desolation for Israel did indeed begin in 609 B.C., then the promised desolation of Israel ended in 539 B.C. with the fall of the Babylon and the decree from King Cyrus of Persia that the exiled Jews could return to Jerusalem (Ezra 1:1-4).

Others believe Israel the 70-year judgment of desolation for refusing to observe Sabbath rest begins with the destruction of the Temple and the Hebrews exile to Babylon in 586 B.C. From the time of the destruction of the Temple in Jerusalem by Nebuchadnezzar II in 586 B.C. to the dedication of the Second Temple by a few of the returning Hebrew exiles in 516 B.C. was a period exactly 70 years. 70 years without the Temple. 70 years without the Temple rituals. 70 years of desolation among the Hebrews. Jeremiah explains, just as the writer of Chronicles did in II Chronicles 36:21, that Israel's 70 years of desolation corresponds to the Hebrews forsaking the 70 seventh year Sabbath rests for those 490 years.

"The whole land will be a desolation and a horror... (until) seventy years are completed..." (Jeremiah 25:11-12).

Wherever you put the starting and stopping point of the 70 years of desolation for Israel--either 609 B.C. to 539 B.C. or 586 B.C. to 516 B.C. -- there can be no denial that God used the Babylonians to destroy the First Temple, to desolate the land, to scatter His people among the nations, and to fulfill His promised judgment against Israel for refusing to rest.

Daniel's Vision of Eternal Rest in the Eternal King through the New Covenant

During the Babylonian exile, Daniel wrote the book that bears his name. Daniel states in Daniel 9:2 that he knew how long Jerusalem would be desolate because he had read Jeremiah:

"I, Daniel, understood from the Scriptures, according to the word of the LORD given to Jeremiah, that the desolation of Jerusalem would last seventy years" (Daniel 9:2).

Then, later in the same chapter, Daniel records an amazing vision that God gave him through the angel Gabriel. It is a vision regarding another 490 years. I'm sure Daniel must have caught his breath when he heard ("seventy sevens") because the desolation Israel was experiencing in his day was a result of Israel's previous 490 year period of refusing to rest. He must have deemed his vision troubling for his nation because it spoke of an additional 490 years of sin, culminating in the final abolishment of the Temple, Jerusalem and the Jewish way of life. Yet the vision included some good news as well. The vision is found in Daniel 9:24-27. In the first verse alone (Daniel 9:24), six things are said to occur by the end of the 490 year time period:

"Seventy sevens (490 years) have been decreed for your people (the Jews) and your holy city (Jerusalem), to (1). finish the transgression, (2). to seal up sin, (3). to atone for wickedness, (4). to bring in everlasting righteousness, (5) to seal up the vision and prophecy and (6). to anoint the Most Holy Place. (Daniel 9:24).

Daniel was told by God in this vision that He would establish a set timetable of another 490 years to "finish the transgression." The Hebrew text uses masculine plural for these seven sevens (490 years) with a singular verb (i.e. "490 years is decreed"). The seven sevens is conceived as ONE UNIT OF TIME. There are no gaps. In the same way the first unit of 490 years of rest refusal was continuous (1095 B.C. to 605 B.C.), so too this second 490 year period of Israel's refusal to rest will be a continuous, single unit of time. God's people had already refused to rest for 490 years and the Jews as a result the Jews found themselves in Babylonian captivity. God came to Daniel while in captivity and said, "This is not the end for 'your people.'" God then set a second 490 year period and said these "seven sevens" or 490 years is decreed for six reasons:

- *"To finish the transgression*." Earlier in the chapter Daniel had prayed to the Lord saying, "Israel has transgressed Thy law" (Daniel 9:11) It is a beautiful prayer (Daniel 9:5-11) where Daniel confesses Israel's sin of refusing to rest in God and violating His Law. To "finish the transgression" at the end of this second 490 years will be Israel's ultimate resistance to, and rejection of, the Person to whom all the Sabbath Laws point-- Jesus Christ. Israel's rejection of the shadow of rest (the Law) was serious and brought temporal punishment at the end of Israel's first 490 year period of sin. Israel's rejection of the reality of rest (the Lord) brings eternal punishment at the end of Israel's second 490 year time period of sin.

- *"To make an end of sin"* or "seal up sins" At the end of this second unit of 490 years (seventy sevens), Israel will complete her transgression against God. Again, their sin during the first 490 year period was a refusal to rest in God. Likewise, Israel's transgression during this prophesied second 490 year period of sin is their continuing refusal to rest in God, resulting in a rejection of the Messiah. Just prior to His death, Jesus said to the Jews, "Your house is left to you desolate" (Matthew 23:38). In the same manner the Hebrews experienced desolation at the end of the first 490 period of Sabbath neglect, so too the Hebrews would experience desolation at the end of their second 490 period of Sabbath neglect (i.e. "the rejection of Jesus, the true Sabbath rest"). This phrase "to make an end of sin" is literally "to seal up sins" and has its fulfillment at the end of the prophesied 490 years when the Jews would reject God's Son and have Him crucified. Jesus said to the Pharisees just prior to His crucifixion, "Go ahead and finish what your ancestors started" (Matthew 23:32).

- *"To make atonement for iniquity."* This is a very clear statement of the cross, the place where "God presented Christ as an atonement for sin" (Romans 3:25).

- *"To bring in everlasting righteousness."* Everlasting righteousness is the result of the at-one-moment and once-for-all death of Jesus Christ for sins (see Hebrews 9:12 and Hebrews 10:10). The atonement of Christ for sins is the ultimate place of rest. "For now the righteousness of God has been revealed apart from the Law" (Romans 3:21). "A righteousness that does not come from my obedience to the law, but that which is through faith in Christ" (Philippians 3:9). The everlasting kingdom of the eternal King is filled with sinners who have found their eternal rest in Him.

- *"To seal up the vision and the prophesy."* To seal up means to "fulfill and confirm" all the prophecies of the Old Testament related to the Messiah (see Luke 18:31). E.J. Young in his classic book The Prophecy of Daniel (Eerdmans, 1949) writes about this phrase "(The word) vision was a technical name for revelation given to Old Testament prophets (cf. Isaiah 1:1; Amos 1:1; etc.) The prophet was the one through whom this vision was revealed to the people. The two words, vision and prophet, therefore, serve to designate the prophetic revelation of the Old Testament period. This revelation was of a temporary, preparatory, typical nature. It pointed forward to the coming of Him who was the great Prophet (Deuteronomy 18:15). When Christ came, there was no further need of prophetic revelation in the Old Testament sense." Jesus Christ "sealed up" the vision and the prophesy of the Old Testament Law and Prophets. All was fulfilled in Him.

- *"To anoint the most holy place."* The title "Anointed One" translates the word Christ (Greek) or Messiah (Hebrew). Jesus the Anointed One experienced His anointing by the Holy Spirit at His baptism and the beginning of His public ministry. "To anoint the most holy place (or one)" is either a reference to the Spirit anointing Jesus at the River Jordan or Jesus anointing the Holy of Holies in heaven when He entered after His resurrection with "His blood" rather than "the blood of goats and calves" (Hebrews 9:11-14). Either way, this sixth item is a reference to Jesus the Anointed One.

The prophecy of Daniel 9:24 states that all six things above are decreed to occur within the 490 years. The next three verses, Daniel 9:25-27 tell us when this 490 year period begins and ends.

The Prophecy that Precisely Predicts the Time of the Coming of the Messiah

Daniel's vision and prophecy (Daniel 9:24-27) that God gave him regarding another 490 year time period (i.e. 70 sevens or 70 weeks of years) is the most amazing prophecy in the Old Testament. It names the date of the Anointed One's appearing. It is most likely the prophecy that sent the Magi from the East to Jerusalem asking Herod, "Where is He that is born King of the Jews" (Matthew 2:2). The Magi, coming from the area of ancient Babylon and Persia, would have been familiar with Daniel's famous prophecy, because for centuries all the trained Magi in the East learned to revere the ancient Jewish seer named Daniel due to his legendary interactions with the powerful Babylonian kings. Once Daniel arrived in the east in 605 B.C., he never went back to Jerusalem. Some believe Daniel is buried in Susa, Iran.

The timetable of Daniel's Messianic prophecy in Daniel 9:24-27 is 490 years (seventy sevens). At the end of Israel's first 490 time period of rest refusal (1095 B.C. to 605 B.C.) there came temporary judgment from God (70 years), but at the end of this second 490 year period of Israel's rest refusal Daniel's vision prophesied an even more severe judgment for Israel because of their rejection of the Anointed One who gives real rest. The first time, Israel rejected the Law (the shadow of reality); the second time, Israel rejected the LORD (the reality of the shadow). Here is the prophecy of the timing of the second 490 year time period given to Daniel by God while in captivity in Babylon.

"(25) So you are to know and discern that from the issuing of a decree to restore and rebuild Jerusalem until Messiah the Prince there will be seven sevens (49 years) and sixty-two sevens (434 years); it (Jerusalem) will be built again, with plaza and moat, even in times of distress. (26) Then after the sixty-two weeks (comes the 70th week) the Messiah will be cut off and have nothing, and (as a result) the people of the prince who is to come will destroy the city and the sanctuary. And its (Jerusalem's) end will come with a flood; even to the end there will be war; desolations are determined. He will confirm a covenant with many (in the) one 'seven.' (27) In the middle of the 'seven,' he will put an end to sacrifice and offering. And on the wing of abominations will come one who makes desolate even until a complete destruction, one that is decreed, is poured out on the one who makes desolate." (Daniel 9:25-27)

The 490 years of Daniel's vision, known as the 70 Weeks of Daniel, begins with "the decree to restore and rebuild Jerusalem." This decree to "restore and rebuild Jerusalem" was given by Persian King Artaxerxes Longimanus in 458 B.C.

458 B.C. is the year when the clock begins for Daniel's 70 Weeks. King Artaxerxes was the fifth Persian king to rule Persian since Cyrus the Great. Artaxerxes was the son of the famous Persian King Xerxes. Sadly, many Christians know very little of Artaxerxes

Longimanus, so named "Longimanus" (Latin) because his right hand was longer than his left. Kids today know of his father, Xerxes, because of the popular movie 300, but Christians should know about Artaxerxes because he is mentioned multiple times in the books of Ezra and Nehemiah.

The dates for Artaxerxes' reign as king of Persia are well documented by ancient sources. These sources include all the Greek historians, Ptolemy's Canon, the Babylonian business tablets, and the Elephantine papyri from Egypt. From these documents, we know that Xerxes was killed in late December of 465 B.C., and the reign of Artaxerxes begins at that time. This is why the decree to restore and build Jerusalem, issued in the seventh year of Artaxerxes' reign, is confidently identified as the year 458 B.C.

The entire decree of Artaxerxes is found in Ezra 7:7-26 and it includes:

a). Artaxerxes permission for "any of the Israelites ... including priests and Levites, who wish to go to Jerusalem with" Ezra, to go (Ezra 7:13).

b). Artaxerxes giving to Ezra large portions of "silver and gold" (Ezra 7:15-16) for the work of restoring Jerusalem. The walls, gates, and roads were all in horrible disrepair.

c). Artaxerxes declaring that Ezra would have "everything he asked" (Ezra 7:7) in fulfilling the decree to rebuild and restore Jerusalem. Thirteen years later when Nehemiah made it to Jerusalem (445/444 B.C.), he was surprised and disappointed to hear that Jerusalem's walls and gates were still in disrepair (Nehemiah 1:1). Ezra had been given by Artaxerxes the authority and the resources to rebuild and restore Jerusalem, but it seems Ezra was too busy with social and religious restoration to get the city rebuilt. With Nehemiah's help, Jerusalem's infrastructure was finally restored.

The 490 Year Prophecy of Daniel 9:24-27 Is Separated Into Three Continuous Time Sections:

1). The first section of time is 7 sevens, or seven weeks of years (**49 years**). Since Daniel's prophecy begins in 458 B.C., the 49-year section has its termination in 409/408 B.C. *when there was the dedication of the restored Jerusalem.* This 49 year period of rebuilding the Temple after the Babylonian captivity is described in the books of Ezra and Nehemiah, the last chronological books of the Old Testament.

2). The second section of time is 62 sevens, or sixty-two weeks of years (**434 years**).This section of time flows immediately after the first section of 49 years. This 434-year section of time covers what is called the inter-testament period (the time between the testaments) and the first portion of the 1st century A.D. The time between the Testaments is the period when sects like the Pharisees and Sadducees and the Sanhedrin arise among the Hebrews. These religious sects picture an ever-increasing Hebrew rebellion against God. Since the 7 seeks of years (49 years) and the 62 weeks of years (434 years) flow as one unit of time, the combined 483 years they total indicate a VERY SPECIFIC YEAR in time. The year the clock begins for Daniel's 70 Weeks is 458 B.C. with the decree of Artaxerxes (see Ezra 7:21). When you begin counting 483 years (a toal of 69 weeks of years) from 458 B.C., recognizing that from 1 B.C. to 1 A.D. there is only one year (there is no year "zero"), you arrive at **A.D. 26** - *the year of Jesus was anointed by the Holy Spirit at Christ's baptism.* **The 70ᵗʰ week of Daniel** begins with Jesus three and a half year public ministry after His baptism. The 70ᵗʰ week of Daniel is not some future time of the anti-Christ, it is the time of the Christ. Jesus' baptism and anointing mark the beginning of the final seven years of Daniel's vision (see below).

3). The third and final section of time is 1 seven, or one week of years (**7 years**). This last 7 years is the final section of Daniel's prophecy and is often called Daniel's 70th Week. As stated above, this last seven years begin with Jesus baptism and anointing. Some

Christians believe there is a massive "gap" of time between Daniel's 69th week and Daniel's 70th week. However, such a large gap of time between the 69th and 70th week of Daniel's prophecy defies logic. God never mentioned to Daniel there was going to be a gap between the 69th and 70th week, and the Hebrew language treats the entire 490 years as one unit of time (i.e. "seventy weeks is determined"). Finally, the first 490 year period (1095 to 605 B.C.) when Israel refused to observe the Sabbath rest corresponds to this latter 490 year period when God decrees He will put an end to His Covenant with Israel because of their refusal to rest. Both 490 periods of time have no gaps.

The 70th Week of Daniel Is About Christ and a Sinner's Rest

The 70th Week of Daniel--the last 7 years of the 490 years – begins in AD 26 at Jesus' baptism and anointing. The 70th week of Daniel continues for 3 and 1/2 years until Christ's crucifixion, and then concludes in 33 A.D. with the stoning of Steven, the first Christian martyr. Right before Jesus was crucified He decreed the destruction of the Temple and the Jews, but the fulfillment of that decree would come 40 years later.

God judged Israel for their 490 years of refusing to rest in His Law of rest by ending His Covenant with Israel. God told Daniel He would end His covenant with Israel "after 70 Weeks (490 years). God is serious about rest. He was serious about it in the Old Covenant. But the person who refuses to rest in the the Christ who has come to inaugurate a New Covenant will experience even more severe judgment (see Hebrews 10:29). And of course, the Jews rejected the Messiah.

Before we look at the judgment that came to Israel for rejecting the Messiah, let's see what happens within or shortly after the 70th Week of Daniel. I will take the events of the 70th week in chronological order of their historical occurrences as we examine Daniel 9:25-27:

- *"He will confirm the covenant with many (in) one seven"* (v. 27).

The "He" here is Jesus Christ, not any anti-Christ. There is nothing in the text that would lead us to believe the He "who confirms the covenant" is anyone other than Messiah the Prince of the previous verse. God makes covenants. This covenant is the New Covenant, the same covenant Jesus described to His disciples when He held up the wine and said, "For this is My blood of the covenant which is to be shed on behalf of many for the forgiveness of sins" (Luke 22:20).

- *"The Messiah will be cut-off and have nothing"* (v. 26)

This is, of course, referring to the crucifixion of the Messiah which occurred 3 1/2 years into Daniel's 70th Week. At His death, Jesus was stripped of all His possessions and buried in a borrowed tomb.

- *"In the middle of the 'seven' he will put an end to sacrifice and offering"* (v. 27)

Christ does this by His death. By the shed blood of Jesus Christ, God put to an end to the Old Testament economy of blood sacrifice and grain offerings. Though the Jews continued with their ritual sacrifices for one more generation, the cross put an end to God's recognition of such. Jesus fulfilled the Law, and never again would heaven appreciate any blood sacrifice that takes the place of God's Son.

- *"Desolations are determined"* (v. 26)

When Jesus cleared the Temple with a whip, overturning the tables of money changers, He said, "Your house is left to you desolate" (Matthew 23:38). This was on Monday of Passion Week. Messiah Prince decreed the destruction of the Temple, the desolation of Jerusalem, and the dispersion of the Jews (Matthew 24), the judgment of God upon the Hebrews for rejecting the Jubilee. The text simply says desolations are determined. The fulfillment of God's decree to desolate Israel would wait 40 years (a generation) and be completed in A.D. 70 by the Romans when Jerusalem and the Temple were utterly destroyed.

- *"And the people of the prince who is to come will destroy the city and the sanctuary"* (v. 26b).

The prince is Messiah the Prince. The people who come to destroy the city and the Temple are His agents. It is no more unlikely that the sovereign God could use the Romans in A.D. 70 to destroy the Temple, the city of Jerusalem and scatter the Hebrews than it is that God could use the Chaldeans, the Assyrians, the Babylonians, and the Egyptians to do the same thing in terms of judgment on His people in the Old Testament. The apocalyptic language of judgment used by Jesus in Matthew 24 as He describes the impending destruction of the Temple and Jerusalem (i.e. "within a generation") is exactly the same imagery used by the Hebrew prophets in the Old Testament to describe the of God judgment on various other nations (see Joel 3:15).

- *"And its end will come with a flood; even to the end there will be war"* (v. 26c).

When Jesus described the coming judgment on Israel in Matthew 24, He said "You will be hearing of wars and rumors of wars... but that is not yet the end." The Romans fought the Jews for nearly three years, and all the way to the very end, when the Temple and the city were finally destroyed, there was war. The reference to "a flood" is Hebrew apocalyptic language used to describe God's judgment and an outpouring of Divine wrath (see Nahum 1:8).

- *"And on the wing of abominations will come one who makes desolate, even until a complete destruction, one that is decreed, is poured out on the one who makes desolate"* (v. 27c).

It is said by Josephus, the captured Jew who served as historian for the Roman general Titus, that when the Romans destroyed Jerusalem and the Temple in A.D. 70, they used pulleys and ropes to pull every stone so that not one was left standing on another.

They set fires to melt the gold and silver in the Temple down, and slaughtered any Jew who did not run to the hills.

This judgment of the Jews was "decreed" by God. It was very similar to the desolation and destruction of Israel by the Babylonians in 586 B.C. The difference, however, is clear. There will never be another Temple built by God. There will never be another sacrificial system reinstated by God. There will never be another favored nation.

Those who rest in Christ are the Temple of the living God. Those in Christ, Jew and Gentile, are "the chosen nation of God." Those who rest in Christ are "the royal priesthood." The New Covenant abolishes the Old Covenant. The New Covenant does a much better job of showing what it means to rest in God by faith, receiving a righteousness that does not come from the Law, but comes from God and is found by faith in Christ.

APPLICATION: *Christ is the Fulfillment of the Law; He is My Jubilee*

God abolishes the Old Covenant Law and institutes the New Covenant through His Son. The Law is only a shadow of the eternal realities that have come in Jesus Christ. Everything in Old Testament Scriptures--the Law, the Prophets, the sacrificial rituals, etc. point to the Messiah. The Anointed One fulfilled the Law, every jot and tittle, and then God abolished the Old Covenant, including all the Sabbath commandments of rest, and now encourages the world to embrace ("kiss") His Son. God's intention has always been to promote the Person who gives real rest, not to crystalize the shadow (the Law) that only prefigured real rest. Legalism is ultimately a turning away from that which is real through the embracing of the picture rather than the Person whom the picture is intended to represent.

When a sinner finds real rest in God through trusting the Person and work of Jesus the Anointed One, the sinner is displaying faith that God will perform a good work--similar to the work of Creation--for sinners, in sinners, and through sinners. This work of God in delivering us from our sins will result in God's declaration of "Very good!" Yes, that's right. God alone takes the chaos of a sinner's life and makes something very, very good.

"For we are His workmanship," (Ephesians 2:10) and "If anyone is in Christ, He is a new creation" (II Corinthians 5:17). The ultimate response to a perfect work of God is rest. The entire intent of God in giving us His word is that we rest in Him! For those of you who wish to work, labor and toil for God's acceptance and love, and find it difficult to rest in God and embrace with joy the fact that God deems you good because you are His work, I would encourage you to realize the seriousness of your dilemma.

If God punished Israel for refusing to rest in Him under the Old Covenant dispensation, "How much more severely do you think someone deserves to be punished who has trampled the Son of God underfoot, who has treated as an unholy thing the blood of the covenant that sanctified them, and who has insulted the Spirit of grace?" (Hebrews 10:29).

When Jesus began His public ministry, He preached his first sermon from Luke 4:18-19. He read out loud for all the Jews to hear:

"The Spirit of the LORD is upon me, for he has anointed me to bring Good News to the poor. He has sent me to proclaim that captives will be released, that the blind will see, that the oppressed will be set free, and that the time of the Lord's favor has come."

The text Jesus read was from the scroll of Isaiah. The prophet was describing the events of the Jubilee year in Israel; events called for by the Law (e.g. release of captives, forgiveness of debts). After Jesus read from Isaiah during his inaugural ministry sermon, "He rolled up the scroll, handed it to the attendant, and sat down. The eyes of everyone in the synagogue were fastened on Him. Jesus began by saying to them, 'Today, this Scripture is fulfilled'" (Luke 4:20-21).

Jesus told his disciples "Do not think that I have come to destroy the Law and the Prophets. I have come to fulfill them!" (Matthew

5:17). Jesus Christ is the reality of rest. The shadow of the Law only pointed to Him. God gave Jesus Christ as an atonement for sin to set sinners free. God gave Jesus Christ as an atonement for sin to forgive sinners' debts. God gave Jesus Christ as an atonement for sin in order to fashion "a new creation," for every sinner in Christ is "the workmanship of God." Just like God rested after the initial creation, He "who began a good work in us will carry it on to completion" (Philippians 1:6), and when it is completed, He will say "Very good. Well done. I am pleased." Why?

Because your deliverance is a perfect work of your God. He never fails.

Rest.

The intent of God in giving us His word is for us to rest in Him. Rest in Christ. Rest in His work. Rest in His performance. Rest in His faithfulness.

Rest.

Rest in knowing you are deemed perfectly righteous because He has given you a righteousness that is not your own and does not come from your obedience to any Law; He has given to you a righteousness that comes from God and is found by rest in Christ.

Rest and then say, "There's no other way!"

Chapter 34: The Good News of the New Covenant Is To Be Lived and Shared

Esther is the only book in the Bible where God's name is never mentioned. That said, Esther is a book where God's grace is uniquely pictured.

Do you see the gospel in Esther?

Esther, the Jewish girl who marries the powerful Persian king, is the heroine. She intervenes on behalf of her people when Haman, a Persian royal who hated the Jews, obtained a Law of the Medes and the Persians - an unalterable law - that all the Jews in the Persian Empire, regardless of age and gender, should be put to death. We, like the Jews in Esther's day, are under a similar unalterable law. "The wages of sin is death" (Romans 6:23). This law is inescapable, regardless of age or gender, fame or fortune, and any attempts to nullify it.

However, seventy days after that first Persian law of death went into effect, Esther intervened on behalf of the Jews to obtain a new law of life (see Esther 8:9), allowing the Jews--on the authority of the king-- to destroy those who sought to put them to death. Since any Law of the Medes and the Persians was irreversible, the new law only made the first law ineffectual, allowing a "way of escape" on the authority of the king. So too, seventy weeks after the Jews were allowed to leave Persia (458 B.C.) to rebuild and restore Jerusalem, Jesus came "to make an end of sin and death" (Daniel 9:24-27) by establishing a New Law (Hebrews 8:13), crushing the head of the enemy of His people (Genesis 3:15).

The new law in Esther's day went into effect with the seal of the king's signet ring (Esther 8:8). The signet ring was worn by ancients and "pressed" into a wax seal to authenticate a document. Interestingly, in Haggai 2:22-23 the Messiah is called "God's signet ring."

"I will overthrow the thrones of kingdoms and destroy the power of the kingdoms of the nations; and I will overthrow the chariots and their riders, and the horses and their riders will go down, everyone by the sword of another. 'On that day,' declares the Lord of hosts, 'I will take you, Zerubbabel, son of Shealtiel, My servant,' declares the Lord, 'and I will make you like a signet ring, for I have chosen you,'" declares the Lord of hosts.

The above verse is a Messianic prophecy that is fulfilled in Jesus Christ. Jesus Christ is God's Signet Ring that authenticates the New Law of life. Often the Old Covenant prophets would promise the return of David to the throne of Israel. Remember, David was the first ruler of Israel appointed by God alone before the exile. But when the prophets of the Old Covenant predicted the return of David, they actually meant "the son of David," for the Messianic prophecies were always about one of David's sons as specifically outlined in II Samuel 7:8–16.

In the same manner, when the prophet Haggai predicted a future King and Kingdom, it was prophecy about Zerubbabel who was the first ruler of Israel appointed by God alone after the exile. Like the prophecies of the future ruler through David's genealogical line, Haggai's words are a prophecy about one of Zerubbabel's sons. So not only is "son of David" a title for the Messiah, so is "son of Zerubbabel." Both Jewish and Christian scholars see the necessity for the Messiah ("God's signet ring") to be a direct descendant of both David and Zerubbabel.

When you read the genealogy of Christ in Matthew 1:13 and Luke 3:27 you find that Jesus Christ comes from the line of King David through Zerubbabel. Jesus is the rightful King of Jews. Jesus fulfills the prophecies of the Messiah as given by the prophets, the King who destroys the power of all other kingdoms. Jesus is God's Signet Ring. The only way the old law of sin and death is rendered ineffective is through God issuing a New Law that protects His people by crushing the head of Satan (i.e. "the ruler of the kingdoms of this world"), a New Law of life that is sealed with the King's Signet Ring, Jesus Christ.

Just as the king of Persia gave his signet ring to Mordecai (see Esther 8), so God so loved us that He gave us His Son (John 3:16 and Hebrews 8), giving Him for our protection (Matthew 1:21) Through the King's Signet Ring (Jesus Christ), the old law of sin and death is made ineffectual. Even though we deserve death each time we sin, God's signet ring renders the irreversible old law ineffectual because Jesus establishes the new law of life. That's rich grace. When we realize what we've been given in the King's signet ring, the riches of the King's grace cause us to lose our desires for the lesser pleasures of this life and to be captivated by the eternal riches of our King (see Ephesians 2:7).
This is the good news from Esther.

Just as the Persian king sent couriers throughout the Persian empire to declare the good news for Esther's family, we are commissioned by the King of Kings to "move swiftly" throughout the world, to go and herald the good news to people everywhere (Matthew 28:18-20). The words of Esther 8:10 (KJV) are specific as to how the couriers went out with the good news...:

 "...by mules, camels, young dromedaries, and horseback."

We who proclaim the gospel can be compared to messengers riding mules. Mules are slow and steady. However, we can also be compared to riders of three faster animals, all mentioned in this Esther text. Camels are faster than mules, young dromedaries are faster than camels, and horses are faster than them all.

It matters not how we get the message of grace out to the world, it only matters that we are riding with an important message. I find it fascinating that the New American Standard lumps all four animals together and translates Esther 8:10 in this manner:

"The king sent out couriers riding on steeds sired by the royal stud."

No mules. No camels. No dromedaries. No horses. Just "steeds sired by the royal stud." Some of our methods may be slow (ever pastor a church that's stuck in the 80's?), some of our methods may be faster than others, (ever been a part of a Christian group that intentionally puts people above programs, and never settles for status quo 'just because we've always done it that way'?), and some of our methods may be swifter than the fastest thoroughbreds (ever been a member of a church that changes their methods for reaching people so fast you can't keep up with the changes?)

If the New American Standard translators are anywhere close to the ballpark in their translation of Esther 8:10, you shouldn't be too quick to judge someone else's methods of carrying the gospel message - whether they're going slow or going fast - for we all are "couriers riding steeds sired by the royal stud." It seems God puts an emphasis on our message and may be a tad indifferent to our chosen methodologies.

I'd like to encourage you to spread by word of mouth the good news of Jesus Christ and the "better promises" that come through faith in Him.

Taking to people the Good News in every possible method available, is the way the Kingdom advances in victory.

When We Understand the New Covenant, We Cease Being Victims.

The New Covenant Scriptures teach us that "In all these things we are more than conquerors through Him who loved us" (Romans 8:37).

Syrian Christians are being tortured, crucified and beheaded in Aleppo, Syria because these Christians are reaching out to their neighbors with the love of Jesus. These Syrians dying for Christ isn't Bible story. It's happening in modern times. Radical Islamicists in Aleppo ordered Christians in their city to leave or face death. These followers of Jesus refused to leave their hometown, choosing to remain in the city to provide aid in the name of Christ to survivors of the carpet bombings.

When the deadline to leave Aleppo passed, these Christians were apprehended, and their torture began. One Syrian Christian father watched as his twelve-year-old son's fingers were cut off. When the father still refused to renounce Christ and convert to Islam, the radicals then beat both father and son, and crucified them with a sign above their heads that read "infidels." During their torture these Syrian Christians sang, prayed for their torturers and displayed super-human inner strength. One eyewitness said the way these Christians died astounded their persecutors. They died as conquerors, not victims.

Meanwhile, we American Christians sip our lattes and nibble our pastries, but find it impossible to overcome the "hurt and pain" we've experienced in life. Most of us can't even spell Aleppo, much less see the difference between the pain and suffering in their lives when compared to ours. We complain about the songs we sing in church, the lack of Facebook likes we receive, and the various ways people disrespect us. We find it easier to point our finger at someone else as the cause of our pain than to look within ourselves to find the reasons for it.

We American Christians have become masters at playing the role of victims.

Jesus said, "Things that come out of a person's mouth come from the heart" (Matthew 15:18). To express "I'm a victim" in life is the ultimate sign of a void within my heart. When I see myself as a victim, I have little or no comprehension of God's love for me in Jesus Christ.

Oh, sure, I may say I understand God's love for me. Maybe I'll even sing about God's love. But the proof is in how I live. When crunch time comes, if I find my satisfaction and happiness in other people, or other things, or in my ability to control life, then I'll play the role of victim. I must play the victim because I am. That in which I trust for my happiness and security has been stolen from me.

Never find the source of your happiness today in what you may lose tomorrow.

I can never lose the love of God. That is the promise of the New Covenant

"For I am convinced that neither death nor life, neither angels or demons, neither the present nor the future, nor any power, neither heights nor depths, nor anything else in this world, will be able to separate us from the love of God that is in Christ Jesus our Lord" (Romans 8:38-39).

If I'm void of a comprehension of God's love for me, then when things get out of control - like a son's fingers being cut off by a radical Islamicists - I'll scream and fight, seek to control and manipulate, lie and steal, look back and payback, and ... well, you get the picture. But when "I know the love of Christ that surpasses knowledge, then I am filled up with all the fulness of God" (Ephesians 3:19).

And when filled with the God's love for me in Christ, then what comes out of me when squeezed by painful events is the love of God. So God will sometimes allow the heat to surround me to reveal the heart that is within me.

Now for the Good News.

God is at work in all His people, turning us from a mindset of victimization to a mindset of being "more than conquerors." The same passage in Romans 8 that points us to the love of Christ trumpets what it means for Christians to be "more than conquerors" in this life. Read it carefully:

"Who shall separate us from the love of Christ? Shall trouble or hardship or persecution or famine or nakedness or danger or sword? No, in all these things we are more than conquerors through Him who loved us." (Romans 8:35, 37).

The little phrase "more than conquerors" translates one Greek word - ὑπερνικ. I'll transliterate the root words of this compound Greek word in English - SUPER NIKE.

Super is the Greek preposition which means more than or superior. *Nike* is the Greek word for victory. Nike is more than a logo; it's a state of mind.

God's love for me through Christ makes me "more than victorious" in my mind, no matter the troubling situation that comes my way in my life.

This is Good News.

The gospel is not just about "going to heaven." It's about being able in this life to be "more than victorious" even when your son's fingers are cut off. It's about having the ability to pray for those who are in the process of actually crucifying you. It's about having the power to be kind to those who hate you and cause you affliction or distress (trouble), famine or nakedness (loss), and danger or sword (harm).

By pointing my finger at someone else as the reason for the loss of my happiness, or the source of my pain, I exhibit a lack of understanding of God's love for me. If I hold someone else responsible for my struggles in this life, I am playing the role of victim and lose any sense of being more than victorious through Christ's love for me.

I must stop it.

For when I rest in the love of Christ - something that no one or no thing can ever take away - I will find that this life's troubles, losses, and painful events only give me an opportunity to show the world that I am more than victorious through Jesus Christ who loves me.

That's the blessing of both believing and resting in the New Covenant.

About Wade Burleson

Wade is a native Oklahoman, born in 1961 in Oklahoma City, but he spent his growing up years in Texas. On the maternal side of his family, Wade is the direct grandson (16x) of Geoffrey Chaucer, the father of English literature. Wade's paternal ancestors (Burleson), also originated in England and came to the Carolinas in the early 1700's. Wade's great-grandfather (7x), John Crawford Burleson (1729-1776) served under George Washington and died in the Battle of Trenton in December 1776.

Wade is a cousin to Rufus Columbus Burleson (1823-1901), former President of Baylor University and Pastor of FBC Houston, and to General Edward Burleson (1798-1851), former Vice-President of the Republic of Texas. Wade's maternal grandfather, F.T.D. Cherry (1912-1970), was an All-American tight end for the University of Oklahoma and a long-time Christian evangelist.

Wade's father, Paul Burleson, served as pastor of eight churches in Oklahoma and Texas from 1950-2007, including the influential Southcliff Baptist Church in Fort Worth, Texas from 1976-1982. Wade's wife, Dr. Rachelle Burleson, DNP, CNS, is a former Hospital Critical Care Manager and former Professor of Nursing at the University of Central Oklahoma. She is now the Chief Nursing Officer at the St. Mary's Regional Medical Center in Enid, Oklahoma. Rachelle received her Bachelor of Science in Nursing from Northwestern Oklahoma State University, her Master's in Nursing from the University of Oklahoma, and her Doctorate in Nursing Practice (2014) from Vanderbilt University in Nashville, Tennessee.

Wade and Rachelle lead travel tours and mission groups all over the world, including Israel, Russia, China, Turkey, Greece, Poland, and England. Wade and Rachelle have co-authored a series on marriage and have taught others how to establish principles of grace in the home through teaching classes and marriage conferences for couples of all ages.

Wade served as pastor of Holdenville, FBC from 1982 to 1987. While serving FBC Holdenville, he completed his Bachelor of Science at East Central University in Ada, Oklahoma, with a double major in Finance and Business Administration. Wade was called in 1987 to pastor the Sheridan Road Baptist Church in Tulsa, Oklahoma. While serving SRBC, he attended Luther Rice Seminary in Jacksonville, Florida. Wade also served as Tulsa Police Chaplain (1987-1992).

In 1992 Wade was called to be the Lead Pastor of Emmanuel Enid. Since Wade's arrival at Emmanuel, the ministry of Emmanuel has grown globally, emphasizing direct mission work in several continents. Wade is a two-time recipient of the Excellence in Broadcasting Award from the Oklahoma Association of Broadcasters. Wade's teaching style is expositional, and he has preached through multiple books of the Bible, verse by verse, including Genesis, Psalms, Daniel, Ephesians, Romans, Galatians, and Luke.

Wade is the President of Istoria Ministries, a 501-C3 non-profit ministry designed *"to reach people with the gospel of Jesus Christ so that His Story becomes the center of all our stories."* He is the author of several books, including the bestselling *Happiness Doesn't Just Happen*. Wade has also written many articles published in professional journals and periodicals. On the Istoria Ministry Blog, www.wadeburleson.org, Wade has written over 2000 articles on theology, history, and current events. He is a member of the Surratt Society, a group of experts on the assassination of Abraham Lincoln. Wade enjoys playing golf and traveling, but his greatest loves are reading books on theology and history and writing books himself.

Wade has been a featured speaker at many conferences for evangelism and missions, history and theology, as well as at preaching conferences. His most requested multi-media presentations on history include:

White Gold: Thomas Jefferson and the Great Salt Plains

A Transient Abode: Abraham Lincoln, John Wilkes Booth, and Boston Corbett

The Greatest Game Ever Played: Carlisle and Army and the Origins of the NFL

Red Earth Courage: The First Secret Mission of the Civil War.

Wade's desire is to be a life-long learner, believing that no person, regardless of his background, should ever grow static in accumulating knowledge. The advent of the information age has made education in all fields–literature, science, theology, history and the arts–available to all.

Wade has served two terms as President of the Oklahoma Baptist General Convention. He has been a trustee of the International Mission Board and currently serves on several non-profit community foundations and boards in the state of Oklahoma. He was appointed by Governor Frank Keating to serve as a regent for the Northwest Oklahoma Board of Higher Education. He was honored by the United States Department of Justice for his work with victim's families during the aftermath of the Alfred P. Murrah Federal Building.

Wade received the Distinguished Silver Star from the Tulsa Police Department for his involvement with a task force investigating crimes that involved the occult. Wade was asked to serve as a consultant to NASA's security office, the Broward County's District Attorney's Office, and the Attorney General's Office in Florida in their investigation and ultimate conviction of John Crutchley, the worst serial killer in Florida history.

Through his involvement with various law enforcement agencies, Wade has ministered to people and law enforcement personnel throughout every major tragedy in Oklahoma since 1987, and he has participated in relief work and ministry after national tragedies, including Hurricane Katrina and 9/11 in New York City.

Wade's passion for reading has led him to become an antiquarian book collector. His favorite books of other centuries include Isaac Newton's *The Chronology of Ancient Kingdoms*; John Gill's *God's Everlasting Love to His Elect;* and Edward Gibbon's *The Decline and Fall of the Roman Empire*. Wade's favorite modern books include Laura Hildebrand's *Unbroken* (the biography of Louis Zamperini), Paul Young's *Crossroads*, and Eric Metaxes' *Dietrich Bonhoeffer: Pastor, Martyr, Prophet, Spy*.

Other than reading, Wade enjoys time spent with friends and family. He learned from Paul Young, a dear friend and author of *The Shack*, a principle that guides his life:

"There is no moment and no person more important than this moment and this person before whom I stand."

The philosophy of life and ministry of Wade Burleson is that of grace. It is his desire that anyone who has ever heard him speak, read his writings, or spent time with him, will better understand God's immeasurable and unconditional grace as explained in *Radically New*.

Made in the USA
San Bernardino, CA
23 April 2017